# COAST TO COAST
## VINTAGE TRAVEL
## IN NORTH AMERICA

# ANTONY SHUGAAR

## CATHERINE DONZEL / MARC WALTER / SABINE ARQUÉ

## THE VENDOME PRESS
### NEW YORK

**ABOVE:** The Mesa Encantada, or Enchanted Mesa, in western New Mexico, a sandstone butte that has long been occupied by the Acoma tribe; photochrom from about 1900.

**OPPOSITE:** Passenger arriving in the New World, illustration from the early twentieth century; Union Pacific baggage tag.

**PRECEDING PAGES:** *Liberty Enlightening the World,* lithograph from the 1890s (page 1); the arrival in New York harbor of the SS *France,* the world's longest passenger ship, on her maiden voyage in February 1962 (pages 2–3); Santa Fe railroad conductor amusing his young charges, bound for the Grand Canyon, 1909 (page 4); the North Coast Limited, which operated between Puget Sound and St. Paul, Minnesota and was one of the first named passenger lines in the U.S., about 1900; its dining car service was highly regarded (page 5).

**OVERLEAF:** Lithography depicting twentieth-century modes of transportation, c. 1910.

# CONTENTS

# TRANSCONTINENTAL
## From Maine to Catalina, Miami to Alaska, by Canal, Steamboat, and Rail

The transformation of Lewis and Clark's trek into the booming transcontinental travel industry of the late-nineteenth century is a fascinating story. In this book, we will attempt to provide a panorama of the continent and the way visitors traveled across it, but let us start off with a description of the evolution of conveyances from the prairie schooner to the paddle-wheeler and the Pullman coach.

That process began with steamboats, and even before that, with canal travel. No one would eagerly take a stagecoach cross-country, but canal packet boats at least offered a smooth ride. Not that stagecoaches were entirely devoid of creature comforts. The Concord stage of the early nineteenth century offered "brilliant decorations and silk upholstery," as Franklin Reck recalls in his classic history, *The Romance of American Transportation*, "There were three seats accommodating nine passengers inside, and room for one more passenger beside the driver on the high seat outside. In these comfortable coaches, the passenger swayed around curves on the swiftest travel then known." Indeed, Reck makes the Concord stage sound almost appealing, but then he reverts to the darker hues in his depiction of travel by coach: "Now and then, a coach pitched over a mountainside, carrying to their death the passengers, horses, and driver."

Canal boats were a much more attractive means of conveyance in some ways, less so in others. They were slow—even the faster packet boats, which were pulled by two horses, instead of the single horse or mule that pulled ordinary canal boats, made just five miles per hour, in contrast to the eight-to-ten miles per hour of the Concord stage—but perhaps that was part of their charm. If a passenger found a packet boat cramped, he or she could hop off onto the towpath and stroll along at the same pace as the packet boat. Things were a little less cheery when it came time to bunk down. There were twenty-one bunks on each side of the average canal packet cabin, for a total for

forty-two berths. Charles Dickens, who traveled by canal boat during his 1842 American tour, recalls: "I found suspended on either side of the cabin three long tiers of hanging bookshelves, designed apparently for volumes of the small octavo size. Looking with greater attention at these contrivances (wondering to find such literary preparations in such a place), I descried on each shelf a sort of microscopic sheet and blanket; then I began dimly to comprehend that the passengers were the library, and that they were to be arranged, edge-wise, on these shelves, till morning."

Those early days of travel were colorful: among the names of popular stagecoach lines were the June Bug line and the Good Intent line; among the names of the relatively fast canal packet boats were the Flying Cloud, the Greyhound, the Lighting, and the Whirlwind.

But it was the steamboat that first made it possible to travel in spacious comfort. And, after Robert Fulton launched the first regularly scheduled commercial steamboat line, up the Hudson from New York City to the state capital, Albany, it was a Roosevelt—Nicholas Roosevelt, great-great-uncle of President Theodore Roosevelt, and a distant relative of FDR—who pioneered steamboat travel on the western rivers, winning a potentially valuable (but ultimately unenforceable) monopoly on steamboat service up and down the Mississippi. The trip was eventful: as the side-wheel steamboat *City of New Orleans* entered the Mississippi, the New Madrid earthquake—the strongest quake ever to hit the continental U.S.—forced the river to flow backward. At one point the Roosevelts moored the side-wheeler to a tree on an island. By morning the island had sunk, and they were forced to cut the line hastily before the fast-disappearing tree branches pulled the steamboat under. They had to contend with vast numbers of migrating squirrels, attacks from Indians in war canoes, convinced that the Roosevelts had caused the earthquake, and—at the end of the trip—a rare Louisiana snowfall.

The steamboat was a major step forward in the process of making travel fast, reliable, and comfortable, but it had its limitations. It could only go so fast—the greatest steamboat race of all time, which pitted the *Natchez* against the *Robert E. Lee* in 1870, was run from New Orleans to St. Louis at an average speed of 14 mph. Steamboats sank, burned, and exploded. And steamboats could run only on an existing river

OPPOSITE: Cunard's RMS *Lusitania* arriving in New York on September 13, 1907, on her maiden voyage.
LEFT: The *Aquitania* steaming out of New York in 1926; nicknamed the "Ship Beautiful," she was the flagship of the Cunard line. Poster by Kenneth D. Shoesmith, c. 1920.
BELOW: Cunard line stateroom baggage sticker.

PRECEDING PAGES: Means of transportation in the twentieth century, lithograph.
RIGHT: Family of immigrants arriving in New York, from Jules Huret's *L'Amérique moderne*, 1911.
BELOW: Dining room of the SS *Kaiser Wilhelm der Grosse*, a German ocean liner of the Norddeutscher Lloyd (NDL) shipping line, launched in 1897.

BELOW: Passenger opening his luggage for a customs inspection in New York harbor, 1909.
INSET: Baggage sticker of the French Line.

network, and only where the water was deep enough and the banks wide enough.

The construction of a transcontinental railroad, with the funding and authorization of the U.S. Congress, began during the Civil War. This was no accident: Abraham Lincoln had been a railroad lawyer before running for president. The construction of the railroad between Omaha, Nebraska, and Sacramento, California, was one of the great sagas of heroism and tales of corruption in American history. The "Big Four" who built the western half of the transcontinental railroad were Collis Huntington, Mark Hopkins, Leland Stanford, and Charles Crocker. Their company, the Central Pacific, managed to build a railroad over the daunting obstacles of the Sierra Nevada mountains. In 1869 a golden spike was driven in at Promontory Point, Utah, marking the meeting of the two railroads—Central Pacific, pushing east from California, and Union Pacific, pushing west from Nebraska. The moment was spectacular. As Franklin Reck narrates it: "The telegraph had kept pace with the roads, and now, on that historic summer's day, the singing wires were to carry to the world the story of the placing of the last tie and the driving of the last few spikes. . . . The tie was a piece of laurel wood from California. . . . Nevada contributed a spike of silver, Arizona a spike of iron, silver, and gold, and California a spike of pure gold. . . . Finally, as the spikes of silver and gold were driven home, the telegrapher signaled each blow of the sledge, and these self-same blows were recorded in every city by the ringing of a bell."

But it was not quite as noble as it seemed. In fact, this is what had happened several weeks earlier: "By the spring of

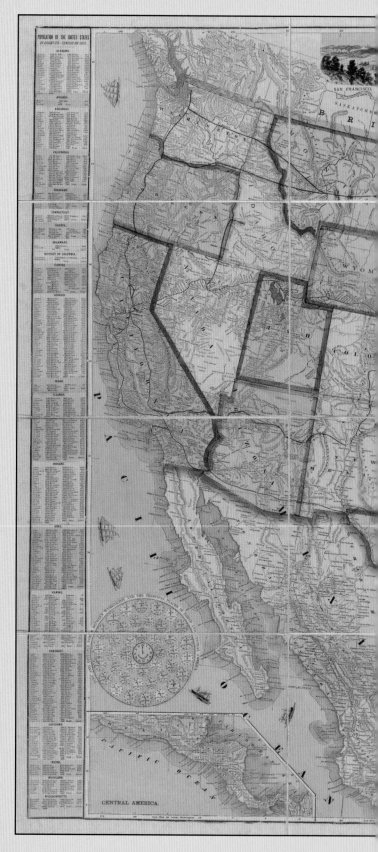

LEFT: *The Great East River Suspension Bridge, Connecting the Cities of New York and Brooklyn,* Currier & Ives color lithograph, 1874. The name *Brooklyn Bridge* had not yet come into use.

ABOVE: Railroad map, published in 1871; in the margins are the populations of the American states, county by county, from the 1870 census.

FROM THE ATLANTIC TO THE PACIFIC OCEAN.

NEW YORK.

1871.

THE AMERICAN UNION RAILROAD MAP

OF THE UNITED STATES

BRITISH POSSESSIONS, WEST INDIES, MEXICO, AND CENTRAL AMERICA.

Published by
HAASIS & LUBRECHT,
107 LIBERTY STREET, NEW YORK.

GULF OF MEXICO

1869 both companies were working in western Utah, Chinese coolies laying track eastward on the Central Pacific, Irish laborers and ex-soldiers sweating westward on the Western Pacific. Day by day they came closer until they were within hailing distance, and finally, on parallel roadbeds, within a stone's throw, they began passing each other, the C.P. blithely laying track eastward and the U.P. as unconcernedly laying track toward the west. It seems incredible, but it is a fact that these two railroads, supposed to effect a meeting, went right on building track as though the other did not exist. In their

13

eagerness to dig into the Federal treasury, both roads apparently intended to keep on building until stopped by the oceans." The reason, of course, was that the federal government issued loans of up to $50,000 per mile of track built.

Ambrose Bierce himself said of the railroad tycoons: "Stanford and Crocker . . . and Huntington . . . are fat, they are rolling in gold, they command all sources and well-springs of power; you've given them houses, you've given them land—before them the righteous all cower."

Whatever darts their envious contemporaries might have launched in their direction, the Big Four helped to make America a single continent, and to launch a convenient and rapid path from one coast to another.

Now, of course, we can travel coast to coast in a few hours. The comfort is debatable, elegance is available as a trade-off against price (amazingly, the penny-per-mile ratio is roughly the same: canal packets cost one-and-a-half cents a mile 150 years ago; now we can fly cross-country for about a dime a mile), and the speed is unparalleled. What is certainly lost, though, is the contact with the countryside.

We once traversed the countryside on canal barges that moved so slowly we could hop off and walk. As the speed increased, we found ourselves leaning over steamboat railings to watch the passing riverbank or seated comfortably at the rear of the train on the "observation platform," watching the world race away from us in a majestic vista of sweeping parallax lines.

Perhaps it was nostalgia for that vanished mode of travel, for that sense of contact with the surrounding scenery, that was at play in a spectacular stowaway case that made the national press in mid-August 1925.

The headline: "Boys Steals Ride on Airship Wing / Young Tramp Makes 300 Mile Trip from Las Vegas, Nev. to Los Angeles / Is Stripped of His Shirt / Admits He Was 'Kinda Dizzy' But Otherwise Completes Perilous Journey Safely."

The article begins: "Los Angeles, August 15, 1925. A boy caught hold of a rising airplane at Las Vegas, Nev. yesterday, clambered upon one of the lower wings, and there rode the 300 miles between the Nevada city and Los Angeles, arriving here none the worse for his thrilling experience except that the wind had whipped the shirt off his back, and the death-defying ride made him, to use his own words, 'a little dizzy.'"

LEFT: Poster for the play *A Mile a Minute*, featuring actress Minnie Palmer.
BELOW: A train running through Animas Canyon, with a view of the Needle Mountains, in Colorado, c. 1900.

OPPOSITE: Passenger in a sleeping car, 1905.
ABOVE: The comforts of a passenger car in 1905.
RIGHT: Dining car in 1905.
INSET, ABOVE: Burlington Route Decal, for Yellowstone Park Via Cody Road, with an image of Buffalo Bill.
INSET, RIGHT: Santa Fe Super Chief baggage sticker, 1938.

LEFT: A 1955 poster by R. Couillard depicting a stainless-steel Canadian Pacific passenger train with scenic domes traveling through the Rocky Mountains. The train ran from Montreal or Toronto to Vancouver.
BELOW: Riders on the New Hance Trail in the Grand Canyon, photochrom, c. 1900.
BOTTOM: Smoking platform at the rear of a passenger train, from Jules Huret's *L'Amérique moderne*, 1911.

TRAVEL
The **Canadian**
THE SCENIC DOME ROUTE ACROSS CANADA
*Canadian Pacific*

OPPOSITE: Sleeping cabin of a Junkers G-24 passenger plane, November 1929.
FACSIMILE: American Express brochure for European tourists. Note the picture of the American Express building at 65 Broadway, built in 1916.

Jack Richman, 17, told reporters he was "hoboing" his way across the country. He said, as transcribed by a journalist who preserved his grammar: "My buddy and me got as far as Las Vegas. We got into there on a passenger train, but they was so many bulls around we had to get out. I came out to the air field and found out about the plane coming here. I thought I'd just take that. I'd rode every other way to Las Vegas. When they started the machine I ran and grabbed hold of the bumper under the end of the wing and stuck on. I got pretty dizzy and kinda sick, but hung on. Then I got up on the wing and kept on stickin' on and got here. That's about all there was to it."

That long-forgotten wing-walk marked the end of a golden era of genteel and vintage cross-country travel.

This book evokes a vanished world. If you're reading it aboard an airplane, you're certainly in the front of the plane. You simply cannot open this book in an economy-class seat. Certainly, Charles Dickens's description of the bunks on a canal boat as "bookshelves" sounds familiar. But by and large the book documents a world of comfortable, spacious travel, across a spacious but rugged continent.

As you leaf through its pages, a world will be revived: a world of ocean liners, from the SS *France* entering New York harbor, escorted by helicopters and fireboats with spraying hoses, to the RMS *Lusitania*. A world of passenger trains with rear platforms, observation domes, and luxurious dining cars and sleeping compartments. A world of cog railways—running up eminences from New Hampshire's Mt. Washington in the northeast to Los Angeles's Mt. Lowe Railway near the Pacific coast. A world of amusement parks, boardwalks, ostrich farms, and alligator ranches. A world in which Niagara Falls—thundering, misting, and even frozen in mid-winter—was one of nature's miracles and not the punch line to corny jokes about honeymoons. A world of steamboat races and steam engines. A world of chateau hotels from one end of Canada to the other; of Flagler hotels, from Florida to Arizona; and of Harvey Houses, staffed by Harvey girls, throughout the Midwest and West. A world of chartered trains, in which moguls and tycoons rode in comfortable private cars from the cities of the northeast to such southern destinations as Magnolia-on-the-Ashley or Georgia's Golden Coast: Sea Island, Jekyll Island, St. Simon's Island. A world of the Old West, extending from Monument Valley and Death Valley to Long Beach, with its beauty pageants and bathing-beauty contests.

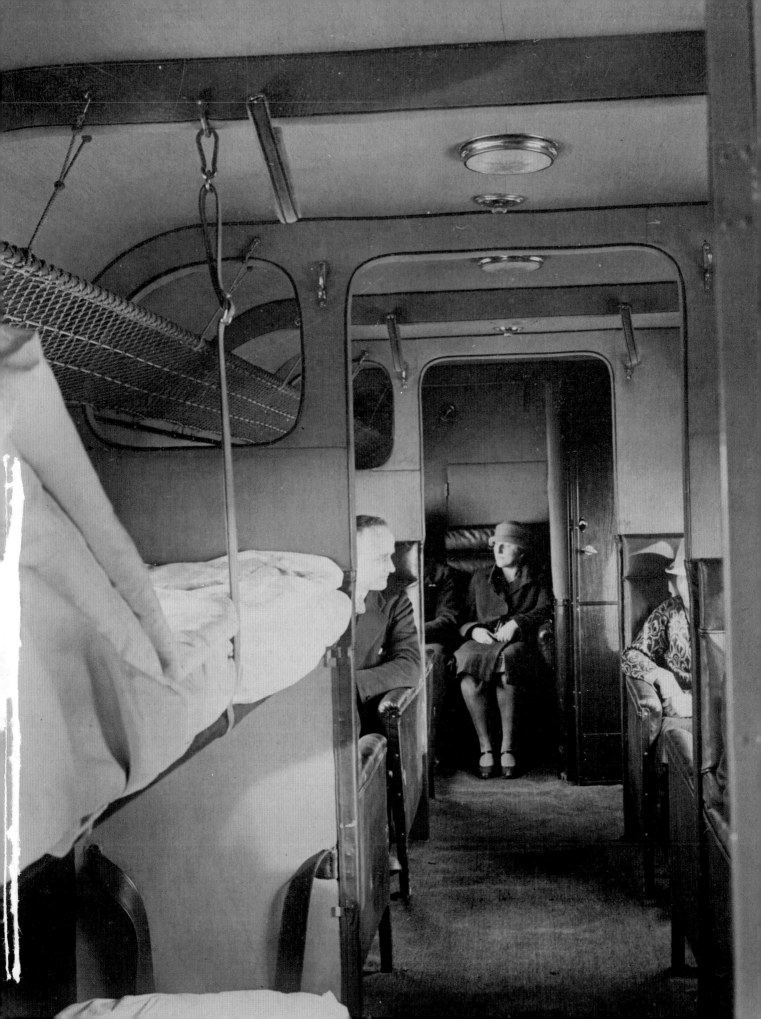

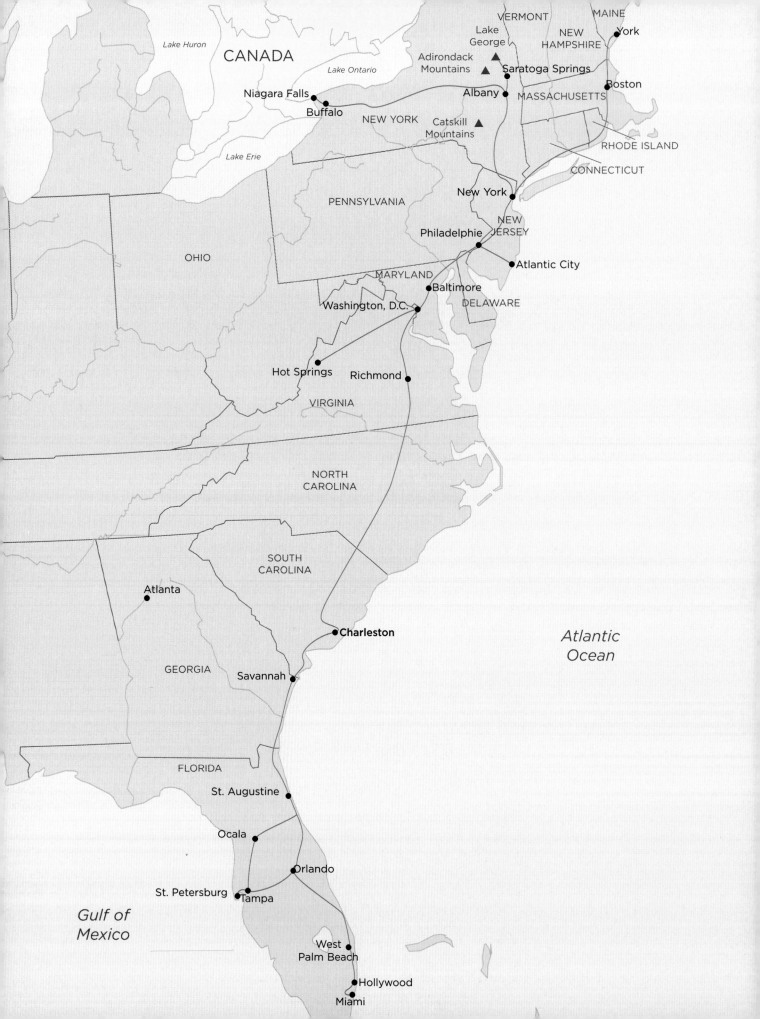

As the nineteenth century drew to a close, travel along the eastern seaboard of the United States—from Massachusetts and New York in the north to Florida in the south—was a mixture of the routine and the adventuresome. The East Coast had been settled to some degree of domestication for three centuries, and yet it had just been ravaged by one of the bloodiest wars the world had ever seen. Travel, largely by rail and steamboat, was thus an act of exploration and a reiteration of ownership.

The idea of travel as a statement of ownership has illustrious pedigrees. The Roman Empire had relatively few walls; indeed, the emblem of its power was its system of roads. Along those roads, the Roman army could move quickly to crush invasions and uprisings. One might imagine the Great Wall of China as an impenetrable barrier to invaders from the north, but in fact it served a major role as a highway, allowing armies to be hurried quickly and safely to points of conflict.

Even now, travel in America is inseparable from security considerations. American families make long and comfortable journeys on the 50,000-mile-long Dwight D. Eisenhower Interstate Highway System, forgetful that it was originally conceived as a network of roads for use by the army in case of emergency or nuclear attack. Popular legend claims—wrongly—that interstate highways have mandatory one-mile straightaways every five to ten miles so that they can be used as landing strips for military aircraft. The railroad in nineteenth-century America had all the military trappings of the Roman road system. Indeed, construction of the transcontinental railroad, crossing North America from Atlantic to Pacific, was begun during the Civil War, in part to bind the Union together.

The various East Coast itineraries explored here knit together the diverse worlds of the earliest English and Spanish settlements of America. Good old Boston, "where the Lowells talk only to Cabots, and the Cabots talk only to God," was for many centuries the queen city of the East Coast. Boston initiated the American Revolution, and—even though it was founded seven years after New York—it always claimed an intellectual and cultural superiority over its grasping and brawling commercial neighbor to the south. But in the early nineteenth century, as the country pushed west to Ohio, Indiana, and Illinois along the southern shores of the Great Lakes, New York seized its opportunity. The Erie Canal provided an

ABOVE: The Towers, an entrance to the Narragansett Pier Casino, Rhode Island, 1890s. The Casino was designed by McKim, Mead, and White.
INSET: Maine Central Railroad's pine tree emblem, 1940s.
LEFT: *West Point, from above Washington Valley Looking down the River,* hand-colored aquatint, 1834, by William James Bennett after a painting by George Cooke.

PRECEDING PAGES: York Beach, Maine, near Kennebunkport, photochrom, 1901.
TOP: Veranda of the Aspinwall Hotel in Lenox, Massachusetts, c. 1920.

inland waterway linking the magnificent ocean port of New York City, via the Hudson River, to the lakes and the interior rivers. New York boomed as its sister cities to the north—Boston—and south—Philadelphia and Baltimore—struggled to keep pace.

Train travel from Boston to New York was a straightforward matter. From New York south, however, passengers had to take a ferry across New York harbor, one of several places where, as one author put it, "rails met the sea." Some terminals required passengers to disembark from their trains and walk aboard the ferries; at other intersections between rail and water, the cars were rolled onto train-ferries, braced into place, and then attached to engines at the far side of the

LEFT: The Great Pan-American Exposition in Buffalo, New York, was an early example of massive nighttime illumination, powered by the nearby hydroelectric generators at Niagara Falls. Photograph by C. D. Arnold, 1901.
BELOW: Engraving of the Canadian Southern Railway running above Niagara Falls, American Oleograph Co.

ABOVE LEFT: This Bain News Service photograph from February 1908 identifies the travelers departing New York by train for Florida as "motorists."
INSET: Mid-century baggage label for the New York Central System.
ABOVE RIGHT: This postcard of two couples riding an elephant in Coney Island's Luna Park was based on a 1905 glass-plate photograph.

water. The experience of rolling stock becoming rolling, pitching, and yawing stock must have been quite a singular one.

One variant on the Boston to Miami run was the journey north from New York to Buffalo and Niagara Falls. The Hudson River Valley offers a succession of magnificent views, which were documented by the landscape painters of the Hudson River School, such as Thomas Cole and Frederic Church. Long before train travel, and even before European settlers, the Hudson Valley was known for its majesty and drama. Charles Mann, in his book *1491*, describes Native Americans plying the river at night in birchbark canoes, by the light of fires set in order to clear the land along the shore for spring planting.

In the late Victorian Era, the idea of Niagara Falls as a honeymoon destination probably involved some thinly veiled sexual innuendo, but there is no doubt that visitors to the spectacular cascades would truly have felt they were at the headwaters of the East Coast: all that water thundering south—and powering electric generators. The Pan-American Exposition of 1901 in Buffalo, a stone's throw from the falls, was a fairytale of electric illumination, one of the first large-scale examples of city lighting, powered entirely by the roaring falls.

If a traveler set out from Boston or New York and headed north to Niagara Falls, he could look southward from a privileged vantage point. Everything that traveler surveyed would be downstream, warmer, and—in South Carolina, Georgia, and Florida—palmier. From the chilly waters cascading into the Niagara River, the train journey would return to New York, cross the Hudson to its western and southern banks, and pass through Philadelphia. The objective of the Confederate Army's summer campaign of 1863—a drive north that ended in catastrophe at Gettysburg—was Philadelphia. The idea was that a Confederate occupation of Philadelphia would have been a shock great enough to force a negotiated peace.

A short detour from the main rail line would take a traveler to Atlantic City, memorialized by Burt Lancaster in Louis Malle's film of that name: "It's a shame you never saw Atlantic City when it had floy floy. Remember the song 'Flat Foot Floogie With the Floy Floy'? Atlantic City had floy floy coming out of its ears in those days." Waxing nostalgic, Lancaster's character, Lou, continues: "The Atlantic Ocean was something then. Yes, you should have seen the Atlantic Ocean in those days."

Nostalgia for Atlantic City in its glory days is certainly understandable. It was a magnificent temple to leisure time, sun, and sand, a more elegant cousin to Coney Island, devoted to "amusing the million." Indeed, Pulitzer Prize–winning playwright Thornton Wilder set Act II of *By the Skin of Our Teeth*, a thinly veiled metaphor for the history of mankind, on the Boardwalk in Atlantic City. (The main character, George Antrobus, is attending a convention at which he will be sworn in as president of the Ancient and Honorable Order of Mammals, Subdivision Humans).

The succession of cities south of Philadelphia—Baltimore, Washington, D.C., Richmond—are the heart of the Mid-Atlantic seaboard. The capital of the Union and the capital of the Confederacy lie half a day's train travel apart, dotting the edge of the great Chesapeake Bay.

The next coastal stop is Charleston, the venerable and somewhat insular capital of the South Carolina sea-trading and rice-planting aristocracy. Charleston—culturally cosmopolitan but socially blinkered—is beautiful, sultry, and luxuriant, though its inland neighbors occasionally toss an envious dart, like this old witticism: "The Charlestonians must be Chinese, because they worship their ancestors, all they eat is rice, and whatever they speak, it's not English." A little farther along the coast is Savannah, Georgia, a city of Spanish moss, antebellum architecture, and two dozen spacious city squares.

This stretch of track was familiar to a number of old-time tycoons. J. P. Morgan regularly chartered private trains, carrying dozens of his close friends and fellow businessmen down to the legendary Jekyll Island Club along Georgia's Golden Coast. Other luxury trains climbed up to the mountains of North Carolina, to estates like the Vanderbilt family's magnificent Biltmore near Asheville in the Great Smoky Mountains.

From the heart of the Old South, the train thunders on into Florida. American popular culture has long romanticized the sleeper-car trip to Florida—in books like John Dos Passos's *The Big Money*, and in movies such as Preston Sturges's *Palm Beach Story* and Billy Wilder's *Some Like It Hot*.

But no depiction of the world of south Florida in its early, booming heyday of wealth and abundance—and brash naïveté—could be as eloquent as the story of the Palm Beach mansion built for an absentee millionaire and designed by a Paris architect. The plans arrived, with all measurements clearly marked, and the mansion was duly constructed. When the architect arrived from Paris with the millionaire to view the finished home, they found that the architect's centimeters had been transformed into the builder's inches, and the magnificent structure was exactly 2.54 times the intended size. Perhaps, in its way, Florida was striving to emulate the mighty Niagara Falls a thousand miles to the north.

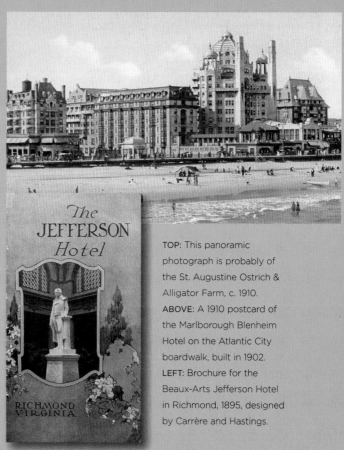

TOP: This panoramic photograph is probably of the St. Augustine Ostrich & Alligator Farm, c. 1910.
ABOVE: A 1910 postcard of the Marlborough Blenheim Hotel on the Atlantic City boardwalk, built in 1902.
LEFT: Brochure for the Beaux-Arts Jefferson Hotel in Richmond, 1895, designed by Carrère and Hastings.

# NEW HAMPSHIRE

ABOVE: A view from the Crawford House in Crawford Notch. In 1909 the *New York Times* reported that social amusements at the Crawford House included bridge parties, dancing, vaudeville shows presented by the "children of the hotel," and burro parties to the summits of nearby peaks. This picture, like the other two pictures on these pages and the one on the overleaf, is a photochrom, or chromolithograph. They all date from 1890 to 1910.

RIGHT: The Mt. Washington cog railway has been climbing the 6,288-foot peak since July 3, 1869. It was the world's first mountain-climbing cog railway.

OPPOSITE: Women playing golf at the Waumbeck Hotel and Cottages in Jefferson, New Hampshire.

OVERLEAF: View of the 800-foot-deep, 90-foot-tall granite-walled Flume Gorge in Franconia Notch, a major mountain pass through the White Mountains.

There are three paths for the ascent of Mount Washington—*one from the Crawford House at the Notch, one from the White Mountain House, five miles beyond the Notch, and one from the Glen. . . . Suppose that we could be lifted suddenly a mile and a quarter above the sea level in the air, and could be sustained there without exertion. That is the privilege we have in standing on the summit of Mount Washington, about sixty-three hundred feet above the ocean. Only the view is vastly more splendid than any that could be presented to us if we could hang poised on wings at the same elevation above a level country, or should see nothing beneath us but "the wrinkled sea." For we are not only upheld at such a height, but we stand in close fellowship with the noblest forms which the substance of the world has assumed under our northern skies. We estimate our height from the ocean level, and it is on a wave that we are lifted—a tremendous ground-swell fifteen miles long, which stiffened before it could subside, or fling its boiling mass upon the bubbling plain. We are perched on the tip of a jet in the centre of it, tossed up five hundred feet higher than any other spout from its tremendous surge, and which was arrested and is now fixed forever as a witness of the passions that have heaved more furiously in the earth's bosom than any which the sea has felt, and as a "tower of observance" for sweeping with the eye the beauty that overlays the globe. It may be that this billow of land was cooled by the sea when it first arose, and that these highest peaks around us were the first portions of New England that saw the light. On a clear morning or evening the silvery gleam of the Atlantic is seen on the southeastern horizon.*

Thomas Starr King, 1859

About 7 o'clock on the warm, moonlit evening of November 9, 1872, *a fire broke out in a building on the corner of Kingston and Summer Sts. It speedily crept up from the lower story and turned the Mansard roof into a sea of flame. The firemen, although heroically active, were driven before it, until early Sunday morning, when several buildings were blown up. About this time the fire was checked in its southward progress, and the whole Fire Department (reinforced from many towns within 100 miles) faced the destroyer on the north. From 2 to 3 o'clock Sunday morning the firemen fought the flames on Washington St., and after incredible efforts kept it on the lower side of the street, and saved the Old South Church, which was scorched and strewn with sparks. During the day the force at hand was directed on two points, the new U. S. Post Office on Devonshire Street, and the Merchant's Exchange, . . . [T]he fire sank rapidly under the cataracts of water which were being poured upon it from the steam-engines massed along State St. By mid-afternoon the danger was over, . . . The best treasure of Boston cannot be burnt up. Her grand capital of culture and character, science and skill, humanity and religion, is beyond the reach of flame. Sweep away every store and house, every school and church, and let the people, with their history and habits, remain, and they still have one of the richest and strongest cities on earth.*

MOSES FOSTER SWEETSER, 1873

## BOSTON

THANKSGIVING DINNER, 1930

Cape Cod Cocktail

Cream of Fresh Mushrooms with Croutons Souffle

Clear Green Turtle

Celery                                    Mixed Olives

ROAST VERMONT TURKEY
Chestnut Dressing          Cranberry Sauce

ROAST BOSTON GREEN GOSLING
Celery and Oyster Stuffing     Apple Sauce

Mashed Potatoes                              Candied Sweet Potatoes

Baked Squash      Creamed Onions     Mashed Turnips

Brussels Sprouts

French Endive—Beet Salad

Hot Mince Pie              Apple Pie              Pumpkin Pie

Frozen Fig Pudding, Melba Sauce
Parfait Nesselrode
Sultana Roll

Black Coffee

Nuts and Raisins

THANKSGIVING

*Ritz-Carlton Hotel*
BOSTON
MASSACHUSETTS

**OPPOSITE:** The Old South Meeting House has an illustrious history. Built in 1729 as a Puritan place of worship, it replaced a wooden meetinghouse built in 1669. Its congregation included such notable members as African-American slave and poet Phillis Wheatley, Benjamin Franklin, and patriot leader Samuel Adams, who gave the signal that started the Boston Tea Party, which was launched from this site. Old South Meeting House made history in the realm of historic preservation as well.  When the congregation moved to Boston's Old South Church, the Old South Meeting House was slated for demolition. Literary figures such as Emerson, Longfellow, and Louisa May Alcott raised a staggering $400,000 in 1870s money and the building was preserved—a model for all later preservation efforts.

**ABOVE LEFT:** The Parker House, shown here in 1925, was founded in 1855 and is the longest continuously operating hotel in America. Charles Dickens gave his first American public reading of *A Christmas Carol* here; many handkerchiefs fluttered at Tiny Tim's death.

**ABOVE RIGHT:** Boston's Public Garden, founded in 1837, was the first public botanical garden in the United States.

**LEFT:** Thanksgiving Dinner menu, 1930, at the Ritz-Carlton Hotel on Boston Common.

268

NEW YORK
Manhattan bridge

THE BRIDGE CONNECTING NEW YORK WITH BROOKLYN HUNG DELICATELY OVER THE EAST RIVER, *and if one half-shut one's eyes it seemed to tremble. It appeared to be quite bare of traffic, and beneath it stretched a smooth empty tongue of water. Both the huge cities seemed to stand there empty and purposeless. As for the houses, it was scarcely possible to distinguish the large ones from the small. In the invisible depths of the streets life probably went on after its own fashion, but above them nothing was discernible save a light fume, which though it never moved seemed the easiest thing in the world to dispel. Even to the harbour, the greatest in the world, peace had returned, and only now and then, probably influenced by some memory of an earlier view close at hand, did one fancy that one saw a ship cutting the water for a little distance. But one could not follow it for long; it escaped one's eyes and was no more to be found.*

FRANZ KAFKA, before 1914

## NEW YORK

PRECEDING PAGES, LEFT: *King's Views of New York*, 1908, featured, on pages 38 and 39, illustrations of two lost masterpieces of New York skyscraper architecture. On the left page of the open book is the Singer Building, completed in 1908, which at 612 feet tall made it the tallest building ever lawfully demolished when it was brought down in 1968. It still holds that record. On the right page is the City Investing Building, which was at the time of its construction in 1908 the largest office building in the world. One Liberty Plaza stands where it once was located.

PRECEDING PAGES, RIGHT: The Equitable Building, built in 1915. It is still standing.

OPPOSITE, TOP LEFT: The Brooklyn Bridge, c. 1900. Completed and opened to the public in 1883, the bridge was originally known as the New York and Brooklyn Bridge, but the name was shortened over time. The granite towers, with their Gothic arches, loomed almost 300 feet above high water in the East River.

OPPOSITE, TOP RIGHT: The Fulton Ferry, made obsolete by the construction of the Brooklyn Bridge. It was founded by Robert Fulton, who pioneered the steamboat; Fulton Street in Manhattan and in Brooklyn were named after the ferry slips on both banks of the river.

OPPOSITE, CENTER: The Manhattan Bridge, opened to traffic between Manhattan and Brooklyn in 1909.

ABOVE: A photochrom of the South Street Seaport in 1900; note the Brooklyn Bridge in the background.

LEFT: Liberty Enlightening the World, generally known as the Statue of Liberty, has stood in New York harbor since 1886; shown here in a 1905 photochrom.

FACSIMILE: Postcard of the docks along the Hudson River, New York, postmarked November 7, 1911.

UNLIKE LONDON AND PARIS, *New York does not possess a number of good old hotels. The old Fifth Avenue Hotel, for instance, was replaced by the Waldorf, which was in turn dethroned by the Plaza and the Ritz. . . . About the middle of the nineteenth century, New York replaced its family boarding houses with the Astor House, and then in 1856 came the Fifth Avenue Hotel, a place of gas-lit luxury, boasting its six floors of white marble and the first elevators; there followed the Commodore, the Brevoort, and finally the Waldorf-Astoria, the opening of which made no less of a sensation that than of the Grand Hôtel in Paris. . . . [U]nder the management of the famous Oscar, the Waldorf-Astoria was the most elegant hotel of the closing years of the nineteenth century. To-day the Waldorf is about to disappear. As with the Pennsylvania, the Belmont, the McAlpin or the Astor (which had the first roof-garden, lit with clusters of gas-jets), the clientèle of the Waldorf is made up of business men and visitors from the country, typically American, and therefore very amusing to observe. The Waldorf hotels still look like diligences, only to be matched by the marvelous padded Montgolfier balloon of the Meurice in Paris. These establishments generally have a prodigious number of rooms, but few sitting-room suites; the organization is military; they don't shine in cooking; morals are strict, as witness the ladies installed behind desks on each floor with an eye on all corridor doors. The reception rooms are palm groves; and here sit gentlemen with hats riveted to their heads, smoking fat cigars from first thing in the morning and expressing themselves with nasal noises; there are telephones on every table, and page-boys stride round bawling room-numbers. In the entrance halls all one's requirements may be found without one having to go into the street; they are like small towns contained within a large room. . . . [Y]ou may enter on any pretext to buy flowers or a newspaper, to eat a sandwich, make an appointment, drink coffee.*

PAUL MORAND, 1930

PRECEDING PAGES: A 1900 photochrom of the Bowery Savings Bank, designed by Stanford White and built in 1895. The building features Corinthian columns, Venetian glass, marble mosaic floors, and 65-foot ceilings. The Third Avenue El (short for "elevated train") lines were built in 1880 and demolished in 1955. The Bowery (as southern Third Avenue was known) had its share of poverty; Stephen Crane's first novel, *Maggie: A Girl of the Streets* (1893), was set here.

OPPOSITE: The 33rd Street entrance to the old Waldorf-Astoria Hotel, in 1902. Note the two elegant women being helped into the horse-drawn carriage. The hotel stood on the present-day site of the Empire State Building, and was built by William Waldorf Astor, nephew of the legendary "Mrs. Astor," queen of New York society.

THIS PAGE, FROM LEFT TO RIGHT: Detail of the Art Deco elevator doors that opened onto the hotel's grand ballroom.

A "belle-hop" at the uptown New York Alamac Hotel.

Postcard depicting Grand Central Terminal, on 42nd Street, then surmounted by the Hotel Commodore, in 1924.

NEW YORK

STREET CLEANERS

SNOW TIMES

CENTRAL PARK ENTRANCE

LEMONADE

23ᴰ ST. AND FIFTH AVE.

FRUIT

MULBERRY BEND

BROOMS AND BASKETS

GERMAN IMMIGRANTS

NEWSBOYS

LUNCH & ICE CREAM

RECREATION PIER

SHOELACES

GREELEY SQUARE

PRETZELS

FREE ICE

CHINATOWN

STATEN ISLAND FERRY

IMMIGRANTS

VEGETABLES

BROADWAY. *Even to those who do not know New York, two names are familiar: one is Manhattan, the other Broadway. Well, if Manhattan is properly speaking New York, the heart of Manhattan is Broadway. This supreme artery gives the island its unity; we have seen it starting off from the Bowling Green as from a bulb, and with perhaps two slight deflections it drives on and on, straight forward, to lose itself Heaven knows where, twenty-five miles away—in the Pacific Ocean perhaps! . . . The canyon of Lower Broadway rings with that noise peculiar to skyscraper streets, for they are more hollowed and reverberant than others, and have a different color too, a color shot through by a grudging daylight, the broken streaks of sunlight struggling through the suspended dust in the upper air. Can they really be called buildings, these straight, clamant cliffs, thrust backward in their uncanny perspectives? They do not scrape the sky, they batter it. Go in amongst them, and it seems as if the perpendicular lines, pressing closer and closer, are pleated together like an accordion, and the parallel lines shoot dizzily downward to meet in a point.*

PAUL MORAND, 1930

BROADWAY THEATRE

KLAW &
ERLANGER'S

STUPENDOUS
PRODUCTION
OF

BEN-
HUR

BY
LEW
WALLACE

DRAMATIZED
BY
WM YOUNG ESQ

PRECEDING PAGES: A compilation of street scenes from a book published by Moses King around the turn of the century. This selection focuses on everyday life of the less well-to-do. Greeley Square is the downtown half of the "bowtie" intersection of Broadway, cutting diagonally across Sixth Avenue at 34th Street. The uptown half is Herald Square,

mentioned in the opening verse of George M. Cohan's 1904 song "Give My Regards to Broadway."

OPPOSITE: Herald Square, looking downtown along Broadway. The Sixth Avenue elevated trains run off to the right. The large building in the foreground on the left is Saks on 34th Street; behind it on the left is Macy's. This section of Broadway was known as "The Great White Way," for the vast amount of electric lighting and the twenty-four-hour-a-day activity.

ABOVE: The Palais Royal on Broadway, late 1920. The dancer Dorothy Dickson, featured on the marquee, sued the owners of the Palais Royal for $10,000 the following year, claiming that she and her dancer husband, Cary Hyson, had a claim to a share of the club's cover charges. And a little more than a year

after this photograph was taken, federal agents were enforcing Prohibition in the club. The owner claimed he was shocked to learn that alcohol was being consumed in the Palais Royal.

LEFT: Vintage poster for an 1899 Broadway production of Ben Hur, a play based on a best-selling American novel of the nineteenth century by Union general and war hero Lew Wallace. Ben Hur was filmed four times.

RIGHT: Times Square as photographed in 1932 by Samuel H. Gottscho, a fabric salesman and part-time photographer who began his career full-time at age fifty, in 1925. His work is now collected in the Library of Congress, Columbia University, and the Museum of the City of New York.

[I]F THE NIGHT WAS MELLOW *I strolled down Madison Avenue past the old Murray Hill Hotel and over Thirty-third Street to the Pennsylvania Station.*

*I began to like New York, the racy, adventurous feel of it at night and the satisfaction that the constant flicker of men and women and machines gives to the restless eye. I liked to walk up Fifth Avenue and pick out romantic women from the crowd and imagine that in a few minutes I was going to enter into their lives. . . . Again at eight o'clock, when the dark lanes of the Forties were five deep with throbbing taxi cabs, bound for the theatre district, I felt a sinking in my heart. Forms leaned together in the taxis as they waited, and voices sang, and there was laughter from unheard jokes, and lighted cigarettes outlined unintelligible gestures inside. Imagining that I, too, was hurrying toward gayety and sharing their intimate excitement, I wished them well.*

F. SCOTT FITZGERALD, 1925

NEW YORK

ABOVE: A 1900 photochrom of New York's Fifth Avenue, looking north from 51st Street. Along the street, note the bell tower of Saint Thomas Church, at 53rd Street (the church burned in 1905 and was rebuilt; it looks slightly different today), and the Fifth Avenue Presbyterian Church, at 55th Street. In the foreground, a pair of twin Vanderbilt mansions (the first is William H. Vanderbilt's home; the second, a mansion he built for his daughters) and the marble château built for William K. and Alva Vanderbilt. This avenue was known as Millionaires' Row.

TOP: Luggage label from the Plaza Hotel, at the foot of New York's Central Park.
RIGHT: The "Limited Express" miniature railway in Central Park, 1904; for viewing in a stereopticon.
OPPOSITE, TOP: The Mall, in New York's Central Park, 1902.
OPPOSITE, BOTTOM: The Plaza Hotel, seen from Grand Army Plaza. The present-day hotel was built in 1907.
OVERLEAF: West Street was the location of several Hudson River terminals for railroad lines heading west and south. Note the footbridges. West Street was later covered by Manhattan's West Side Highway.

## THE GRANDEST PALACE DRAWING ROOM STEAMERS IN THE WORLD.
## DREW AND ST. JOHN.
## OF THE PEOPLE'S NEW YORK & ALBANY EVENING LINE.
### PASSING ON THE HUDSON.

LEAVE NEW YORK DAILY
6 P.M.
From Pier H. N.R. foot of Canal St.
CONNECTING AT ALBANY WITH EXPRESS
TRAINS FOR SARATOGA, LAKE GEORGE,
LAKE CHAMPLAIN, THE ADIRONDACKS,
MONTREAL & POINTS NORTH & WEST.

LEAVE ALBANY EVERY EVNG
8 o'Clock.
ON ARRIVAL OF TRAINS;
MAKING CLOSE CONNECTION AT
NEW YORK WITH TRAINS FOR
PHILADELPHIA, BALTIMORE,
WASHINGTON & THE SOUTH.

THEY DREW UP BEFORE THE FANTASTICALLY COLUMNED ENTRANCE OF THE UNITED STATES HOTEL. *The three passengers in Bartholomew Van Steed's equipage stared in stunned disbelief at a sight which could be duplicated nowhere else in America—or in the world, for that matter. Slim columns rose three stories high from a piazza whose width and length were of the dimensions of a vast assembly room. A gay frieze of petunias and scarlet geraniums in huge boxes blazed like footlights to illumine the bizarre company that now crowded the space on the other side of the porch rail. . . . Up and down, up and down the length of the enormous piazza moved a mass of people, slowly, solemnly, almost treading on each other's heels. The guests of the United States Hotel were digesting their gargantuan midday meal. . . . Here, in July, were gathered the worst and the best of America. . . . Here, for three months in the year, was a raffish, provincial and swaggering society; a snobbish, conservative, Victorian society; religious sects meeting in tents; gamblers and race-track habitués swarming in hotels and paddocks and game rooms. Millionaires glutted with grabbing, still reaching out for more; black-satin madams, peroxided and portly, driving the length of Broadway at four in the afternoon, their girls, befeathered and bedizened, clustered about them like overblown flowers. Invalids in search of health; girls in search of husbands. Politicians, speculators, jockeys; dowagers, sporting men, sporting women; middle-class merchants with their plump wives and hopeful daughters; trollops, railroad tycoons, croupiers, thugs: judges, actresses, Western ranchers and cattle men. Prim, bawdy, vulgar, sedate, flashy, substantial. Saratoga.*

EDNA FERBER, 1941

## HUDSON RIVER VALLEY

**OPPOSITE:** A striking Currier & Ives print from 1878 shows two side-wheel river steamboats heading up and down the Hudson River, respectively. The boats provided "red plush and tassel overnight service" between New York City and the state capital, Albany. A journalist who traveled to Albany aboard the *Drew* that same year described "the pale moonlight, and the larboard and starboard lights, and the blazes from the great furnaces that dot the eastern shore."

**ABOVE:** The Poughkeepsie Railroad Bridge, a cantilever structure built in 1889, was the main railroad crossing over the Hudson River when this photograph was taken in 1904; great

iron mills with their furnaces lined the shore there. The reporter on board the *Drew* described the scene: the flames pouring from the tops of the chimneys, the molten iron running about the floor in streams, "half-naked devils" working it with long-handled tools.

**TOP LEFT:** An 1890 photograph of Fleischmann's Station, on the Ulster and Delaware line in the Catskills. It is still in use.

**BOTTOM LEFT:** The town of Saratoga Springs was a popular spa in the nineteenth century; life there was immortalized in Edna Ferber's *Saratoga Trunk*, later made into a film with Gary Cooper and Ingrid Bergman.

As the lake begins to contract to a river, *it would seem as though the land disputed its onward progress, and in the struggle for supremacy the resistless current has broken the firm earth into a thousand fragments, some larger, some smaller, which vainly endeavor to entangle the waters in their downward course to the sea. . . . The islands number more nearly two thousand than one, and are of every conceivable size, shape and appearance, from the merest dot on the water to an extensive tract of many acres. "At times the steamer passes so close to these islands that a pebble might be cast on their shore; while looking ahead, it appears as though further progress were effectually barred. Approaching the threatening shores, a channel suddenly appears, and you are whirled into a magnificent amphitheatre of lake that is, to all appearance, bounded by an immense green bank. At your approach the mass is moved as if by magic, and a hundred little isles appear in its place." As the journey progresses, the vision is greeted, not by castles in ruins, as in a tour of the Rhine, but by the view of castellated towers in modern architecture, in a most comfortable state of repair, being the summer homes of some of America's celebrities.*

Grand Trunk Railway Company, 1895

## LAKE GEORGE ADIRONDACKS

ABOVE: Tourists on a double-decker boat, nearing the south end of Blue Mountain Lake, in the Adirondacks (1911). Note the photographer on the upper deck, taking a picture of the photographer on the dock.

TOP LEFT: This 1904 photochrom shows the dock of the Sagamore, a grand Victorian hotel on the privately owned Green Island in Lake George, at the base of the Adirondack Mountains in New York.

TOP RIGHT: A 1903 photochrom shows "an open Adirondack camp," a three-sided lean-to that became nationally popular after one was exhibited at the 1876 Philadelphia Centennial Exposition.

LEFT: A pamphlet publicizing the Thousand Islands, an archipelago of islands near the New York-Canada border. George Boldt, who managed the Waldorf-Astoria Hotel, built Boldt Castle on one of the Thousand Islands, and popularized the salad dressing of that name by having it served at his hotel.

OPPOSITE: "An Adirondack Carry," reads the title of this 1902 photochrom. The phrase was a standard expression for portaging canoes.

OVERLEAF: Turn-of-the-century picnickers.

FACSIMILE: Tourist brochure for High Falls Gorge in the Adirondacks, where the Ausable River descends 700 feet in a series of waterfalls between granite cliffs.

HIGH
FALLS
GORGE

In the Adirondacks

LIGHT AND ATMOSPHERE ARE MAGICIANS *who take time to show us all the phases of any landscape, and at Niagara their interpretations are peculiarly important. The evening of our first day by the falls will differ greatly from its morning; neither will be quite like the evening or the morning of any other day; and yet some indispensable aids to appreciation may be long postponed. There must be strongest sunshine to show the full glory of the place—the refulgent possibilities of its opaline falling sheets, snow-white rising mists, and prismatic bows. But only a soft gray light can bring out the local colors of its horizontal waters and its woodlands, and only the shadow of storm-clouds the vehement temper of some portions of its rapids. Night brings her own revelations—lambent, ineffable in the full, and occult, apocalyptic in the dark of the moon. Again, a wind is needed to raise the clouds from the cataracts in fullest volume, and to whip the crests of the rapids into farthest-flying scud. But if it blows too strongly it dissipates the clouds and flattens the white crests, and may drive us back from some of the best points of view, drenched and blinded by torrents of vapor.*

MRS. SCHUYLER VAN RENSSELAER, 1901

# NIAGARA FALLS

**ABOVE:** An 1876 lithograph of the suspension bridge over Niagara Gorge. As a novel first step in the construction of the bridge, a kite-flying contest was held. Fifteen-year-old Homan Walsh successfully flew his kite across the river and collected a $5 prize. A stronger line was then attached to the kite string and pulled across, followed by a rope, a 36-strand cable, and eventually, the bridge itself.

**OPPOSITE:** A 1900 photochrom of the smaller American Falls and the biblically named Rock of Ages.

**OVERLEAF:** Ice formations on the falls about 1890.

**ABOVE:** Horseshoe Falls, shown in 1910, is the most spectacular set of falls on the Niagara River. The curved wall of water is mostly on Canadian territory, but this photograph was taken from American soil, on Goat Island. The reliably irreverent Mark Twain memorably wrote about tourist photographs at the falls: "There is no actual harm in making Niagara a background whereon to display one's marvelous insignificance in a good strong light, but it requires a sort of superhuman self-complacency to enable one to do it."

SANSOM STREET, BELOW NINTH, *runs a modest course through the middle of the afternoon, scooped between high and rather grimy walls so that a coolness and a shadow are upon it. It is a homely little channel, frequented by laundry wagons taking away great piles of soiled linen from the rear of the Continental Hotel, and little barefoot urchins pushing carts full of kindling wood picked up from the litter of splintered packing cases. . . . And then we saw a little oyster café, well known to many lovers of good cheer, that has been furbishing itself for the jolly days to come. . . . The little café has repainted its white front so that it shines hospitably; and the sill and the cellar trapdoor where the barrels go in, and the shutters and the awning poles in front, are all a sticky, glistening green. . . . When the cold winds begin to harp and whinney at street corners and wives go seeking among camphor balls for our last year's overcoats, you will be glad to resume your acquaintance with a bowl of steaming bivalves, swimming in milk with little clots of yellow butter twirling on the surface of the broth. An oyster stew, a glass of light beer and a corncob pipe will keep your blue eyes blue to any weather, as a young poet of our acquaintance puts it.*

CHRISTOPHER MORLEY, 1920

## PHILADELPHIA

ABOVE: Philadelphia's South Broad Street, looking north toward City Hall, in a 1901 photochrom.

RIGHT: The Benjamin Franklin Hotel, familiarly known as the Ben Franklin House, or—even shorter—the Ben, was built in 1925, and featured one of Philadelphia's largest ballrooms. The hotel boasted 1,200 guest rooms and stood eighteen stories tall. The three-tower structure brought light and air to every room.

OPPOSITE: The Hotel Walton, in about 1890.

OVERLEAF: This turn-of-the-century photochrom depicts the Riverside Drive, along the Delaware Water Gap, in Delaware. A venerable canoeing and hiking area, the Delaware Water Gap lies along the border between New Jersey and Pennsylvania, where the Delaware River cuts through the ridge of the Appalachian Mountains. The distinctive land formation of the gap can be seen in the distance.

JUST WHAT PEOPLE DO IN ATLANTIC CITY *is a mystery to anyone who comes here to observe. Some undoubtedly come to rest and enjoy the wide beach and the Boardwalk and the sunshine, and to sleep to the sound of surf. Visitors are old and middle-aged and young. To watch their mass comings and goings is like watching a swarm of bees, or rather ants, for they are perpetually restless, and they are everywhere. But somehow there is always plenty of room, at least outdoors, and on the big piers where much of the entertainment is centered. It is one of the peculiarities of these piers that the price of admission pays for the privilege of enjoying everything on them, except, of course, food and drink. One can go to two or three theaters in succession . . . or dance or look at the circus or sea, or bask in deck chairs, and only pay what is required at the entrance. This policy is as unusual as the rolling chairs on the Boardwalk, which have never been popular or profitable anywhere else. Probably the reason is that the length of the Boardwalk is so appalling that only the hardiest of young legs can cover it from end to end.*

HERBERT RUSSELL, 1947

**OPPOSITE, TOP:** The Atlantic City boardwalk was one of the great attractions of the East Coast. This photochrom from the turn of the century was probably taken during the cooler months: note the overcoats. It was copyrighted in 1900, just two years before a terrible fire devastated the entire boardwalk.

**OPPOSITE, BOTTOM LEFT AND RIGHT:** Atlantic City by night, turn-of-the-century postcards. Left, the Breakers Hotel. Right, Young's Million Dollar Pier, an amusement park built in 1906; its address was No. 1, Atlantic Ocean, Atlantic City, NJ.

**ABOVE:** The artistic impulse expressed itself in sand, and in socially progressive slogans ("Don't Forget the Workers").

**LEFT:** A crowded summertime Atlantic City beach scene. Note the advertisement for baseball at Inlet Park on the cloth covering the horse that pulls the ice cream wagon.

**OVERLEAF:** This 1910 photograph shows a crowd on the beach by the Steel Pier. One of the attractions at the Steel Pier, which opened in 1898, was the "high-diving horses." The horses would dive, with their rider, from a tower originally sixty feet high, though later shortened to thirty feet.

### THE WHITE HOUSE

● The White House has been the home of the Presidents from the time of John Adams to the present. Washington selected the site, laid the cornerstone in 1792, and with his wife, Martha, inspected the finished building in 1799. The building is of Virginia Freestone. After the house had been fired by British troops in 1814 and only the walls were left standing, the restored exterior was painted white to obliterate the marks of the fire.

### BLAIR-LEE HOUSE AND BLAIR HOUSE

● The Blair-Lee House and the Blair House are official guest houses of the Nation. When a visiting dignitary occupies one of the houses, his Nation's flag always appears on the mast. There are no flags when the houses are not in use. President Truman occupied the Blair House during the White House renovation, 1948-1951. The American flag was on the Blair House mast whenever President Truman was in the city.

THE WHITE HOUSE — SOUTH SIDE

THE AIR IS HEAVY, THE HEAT STIFLING, THE DUST AND THE MOSQUITOES PURSUE YOU WITHOUT MERCY. *"Arlington House," that great hotel patronised by the official world, the rendezvous of senators, politicians, lawyers, who swarm there, is certainly the least agreeable of all the great caravanserais of the New World. I am spending sleepless nights stifling under a mosquito net which has the fault of not being impervious to my tormentors, and whiling away the hottest hours of the day in the rooms on the ground-floor of the house, or on the veranda. Stretched out on easy-chairs are a multitude of other men, striving in like manner to pass the most intolerable part of the day in the most comfortable way possible. They smoke, they spit, they fix their eyes on the ceiling, but they won't talk. A dead silence pervades the whole place.*

BARON DE HÜBNER, 1871

# WASHINGTON, D.C.

OPPOSITE, TOP: A two-page spread from a 1950s souvenir booklet. The photographs are of the north façade of the White House, the Blair-Lee House and Blair House (where President Truman lived while the White House was undergoing renovation in 1948–51), and the south façade of the White House.

OPPOSITE, BOTTOM: A photograph of the bar in the Willard Hotel in the first decade of the twentieth century. The author Nathaniel Hawthorne once said that "the Willard Hotel more justly could be called the center of Washington than either the Capitol or the White House or the State Department."

ABOVE LEFT: The cover of the souvenir brochure.

ABOVE RIGHT: A page featuring the Lincoln Memorial and the Lincoln Museum, the old Ford's Theater.

LEFT: The Mayflower Hotel, nicknamed "the Grande Dame of Washington," has been the site of an inaugural ball following every election since Calvin Coolidge re-took the oath of office as president in 1925 (true to form, the antisocial Coolidge failed to show up for his own inaugural ball).

HOT SPRINGS, VIRGINIA

ABOVE: Mounts, carriages, and riders outside the porte cochere and veranda of the Homestead Hotel, in Hot Springs, Virginia. This venerable luxury hotel has hosted presidents and kings. It was purchased by a consortium led by J. P. Morgan in 1888. In 1915 President Woodrow Wilson honeymooned here with his second wife, Edith Galt Wilson. Other guests have included presidents Taft, Coolidge, Hoover, Roosevelt, Truman, Eisenhower, Nixon, Johnson, Carter, Reagan, Ford, and Bush.

OPPOSITE, LEFT: The logo of the C&O Railroad featured Chessie, a kitten. The full slogan first appeared in an ad in *Fortune* magazine in 1933: "Sleep Like a Kitten and Wake Up Fresh as a Daisy in Air-Conditioned Comfort."

OPPOSITE, RIGHT: Tennis match at the Homestead.

LEFT: Turn-of-the-century postcard.

To say that St. Simon's Island is the most famous twelve miles of land surrounded by water *in the Atlantic Ocean is to make a statement strictly in accordance with truth. With what other small patch of territory in Western waters is associated so many great people, whose names are household words in modern history?*

*What other pinch of a paradise, gleaming in the Western seas, can make claims to association with such famous people as Gen. James Oglethorpe, who lived longer on earth than any other English general ever did; as John Wesley, the greatest preacher since St. Paul; Charles Wesley, who wrote more hymns than any other man in the Christian centuries; John Bartram, the greatest natural botanist of his time, according to Linnaeus ; Sir Charles Lyell, the founder of modern geology; Oliver Goldsmith, the friend of Dr. Samuel Johnson; Nathaniel Greene, the greatest general, after Washington, in the Revolutionary War; "Light-Horse Harry" Lee, the father of Robert E. Lee, the greatest general America ever produced; Eli Whitney, the inventor of the cotton gin; Fannie Kemble, the most accomplished woman of the Nineteenth Century; Owen Wister, one of America's greatest novelists; Sidney Lanier, who wrote the "Marshes of Glynn," the greatest poem ever written by an American, which he wrote to celebrate the waters surrounding St. Simon's Island; Aaron Burr, vice-president of the United States and grandson of Jonathan Edwards; Hon. Amelia M. Murray, one of Victoria's maids of honor, and Frederika Bremer, the most popular Swedish novelist of her time.*

James Wideman Lee, 1920

# GEORGIA

**PRECEDING PAGES:** A turn-of-the-century photochrom of the Drayton family plantation, Magnolia-on-the-Ashley. The Ashley River runs through Charleston, South Carolina, and forms the city's harbor. When Margaret Mitchell named her character Ashley Wilkes, she had in mind both the river and the aristocratic Southern family after whom the river was named. Note the Spanish moss draping the ancient trees.

**ABOVE:** Howard Coffin, an automobile executive and aviation pioneer, was the developer of Sea Island, Georgia, and the other "Golden Isles": Jekyll Island, St. Simons Island, and Little St. Simons Island. He built an exclusive hotel, the Cloister, on Sea Island.
**LEFT:** The interior of the hotel in the 1920s.
**INSET:** African-American women seated on the steps of a building at Atlanta University. This photograph was taken by black photographer Thomas Askew, and was part of the collection of W.E.B. Du Bois. It was exhibited at the 1900 Exposition Universelle in Paris.

WE HAVE BEEN HAVING A GREAT TIME HERE. *Mr. Flagler, the proprietor of the Ponce de Leon, seems to have singled me out for his courtesies. I have been with him all day, and he is sitting by me now, while I am writing. He has made some wonderful changes here, so they say, and an Englishman who has been all over the world says that the Ponce de Leon is the finest hotel in the world, being a combination of the good points of all. . . . [Flagler] seemed to take to me, and addressed himself almost wholly to my ears as he showed us over the hotel. He carried us into the grand parlor, and began to expatiate on the cost of the paintings. One was especially voluminous in price. "Yes," said I, "it is certainly fine, but where is the bar-room?" He must have thought I was after liquor, instead of trying to call him away from the price of the pictures. I judge he has never forgotten the episode. You see the cornfield journalist ruined himself with the author and inventor of crude petroleum and Ponce de Leon hotels.*

JOEL CHANDLER HARRIS, 1890–98

## ST. AUGUSTINE

BOTTOM LEFT: A 1938 Parks Service poster for Fort Marion, as the Castillo de San Marcos was known until 1942. The fort was built in the 1670s; St. Augustine itself was founded in 1565.
ABOVE: A woman writing a letter in a luxurious drawing room in the Ponce de Leon Hotel, also built by Flagler, across the street from the Alcazar.
OPPOSITE: Lunch menu from the Ponce de Leon Hotel for February 27, 1880.
OVERLEAF: In this 1886 photograph by renowned landscape photographer George Barker, a steamboat approaches the dock of the Morgan House, a hotel in Silver Springs, Florida. Tourists traveling to Silver Springs before the railroad was built would board a steamer south of Jacksonville and navigate the brown waters of the Ocklawaha River and a thickly forested swamp until they reached the crystal-clear waters that poured out of the "silver" springs.

PRECEDING PAGES: The Alcazar Hotel in St. Augustine, Florida, depicted in an 1898 photochrom. The hotel was founded by Henry Flagler, an oil tycoon and real estate developer (and the father of Miami Beach), to house wealthy tourists riding south on his railroad. It was built in 1887 in the Spanish Renaissance style, and was one of the earliest poured-concrete buildings in the world.
ABOVE: When the Alcazar Hotel was built, it housed the world's largest indoor swimming pool. The building now serves as a museum and as St. Augustine's City Hall.

# HOTEL PONCE DE LEON

O·D· Seavey, Manager,
## St. AUGUSTINE,
### FLORIDA.

## Lunch.

**WEDNESDAY, FEBRUARY 27, 1889.**

Rice Lié, à l'Allemande.          Consommé en Tasse.

Broiled Shad, Maître d' Hôtel.
*Radishes.*                    *Potatoes, Dauphines.*

Roast Ribs of Beef.          Lamb Ballotine, à l' Espagnole.
*Mashed Potatoes.*          *Stewed Tomatoes.*

Crab Croquettes, à la Crême.
Small Sirloin, à la Cheron.
*White Beans aux Fines Herbes.*   *New Potatoes.*   *Russian Turnips.*
Pork and Beans, Boston style—Hot Boston Brown Bread.

Ribs of Beef.      Mutton.      Ham.      Pickled Tripe.
Pickled Lamb's Tongue.          Pressed Corned Beef.
Pickled Eel.          Tongue.

THE
SPANISH-MORESQUE PALACES
ST. AUGUSTINE, FLORIDA.
HOTEL CORDOVA.          HOTEL ALCAZAR.

FLORIDA, FOLKS! *Singing, dancing and entertainment! After the entertainment, there'll be sandwiches. But, remember, if there are no lots sold, there'll be no sandwiches. Florida, folks! Sunshine, sunshine! Perpetual sunshine all the year around! Let's get the auction started before we get a tornado. Right this way. Step forward, everybody. Friends, you are now in Cocoanut Manor, one of the finest cities in Florida. Of course, we still need a few finishing touches, but who doesn't? . . . Eight hundred wonderful residences will be built right here. Why, they're as good as up. Better. You can have any kind of a home you want to. You can even get stucco—Oh, how you can get stuck-o! Now is the time to buy while the new boom is on. Remember that old saying: "a new boom sweeps clean" and don't forget the guarantee—my personal guarantee: If these lots don't double in value in a year, I don't know what you can do about it. Now then, we'll take lot number twenty—lot number twentah—right at the corner of DeSoto Avenue. . . . Now what am I offered for this lot? Anything at all? Anything at all? . . . Sold for six hundred dollars. Wrap up that lot and put some poison ivy on it.*

MORRIE RYSKIND, 1929

## PALM BEACH

OPPOSITE: A woman and a couple ride in a Palm Beach version of a rickshaw, described as "bicycle buggies," about 1900. The men behind the chairs are riding pedal bikes.

ABOVE: The Royal Poinciana Hotel of Palm Beach in 1900, another of Henry Flagler's creations (construction began in 1893).

LEFT: The Great Southern Hotel was built in 1924 in Hollywood, Florida (just north of Miami Beach). In 1926 the *Literary Digest* illustrated the new tourist mecca; that magazine was a popular national weekly until the late 1930s, when it merged into *Time*.

OVERLEAF: The Royal Poinciana Hotel on Lake Worth, Palm Beach, was built in the last decade of the nineteenth century by visionary oil tycoon, railroad magnate, and real estate developer Henry Flagler. The gardens of the hotel offered shade to the guests and the restful sound of palm trees in the sea breezes.

THE [NEW YORK] SUN'S ACCOUNT OF SOUTH FLORIDA COASTAL LIFE IN THE 1870'S *shows both a rosy and a grim side. There were rattlers, panthers, alligators and no shortage of mosquitoes. But fresh venison could be purchased from the Seminoles for a few beads, bear steak was plentiful, gigantic sea turtles walked right up to the dinner table and, of course, the climate and fishing were superlative. . . . [But] if a person wanted to send a letter the ninety miles from Miami north to Jupiter, he had to put it on the Key West mail schooner. It then went to Cuba, was taken by steamer to New York and finally came back down to the lighthouse community by train and Indian River boat. As long as two months and three thousand miles were required to send a letter less than one hundred miles. The government started the famous barefoot mailman route. The only road was the beach and, for $300 a year, a mailman walked what became a regular route between Palm Beach and Miami. He walked barefoot because that's the easiest way to walk on hard, wet sand.*

STANLEY JOHNSON AND PHYLLIS SHAPIRO, 1987

# MIAMI

OPPOSITE: The Hollywood Beach Hotel, completed in 1926, was designed by Addison Mizner. The Mizner brothers, Addison and Wilson, had aristocratic forebears—they were descended from Joshua Reynolds—but they were rogues and wits. They swindled tycoons in boomtown Florida throughout the 1920s. Two of Wilson Mizner's better known lines are: "You sparkle with larceny," and "Always be nice to people on the way up because you'll meet the same people on the way down." The 2003 Stephen Sondheim musical *Bounce* is based on the lives of the Mizner brothers.

ABOVE: Miami's Royal Palm Hotel in 1900. Built by Henry Flagler in 1897, the Royal Palm featured the city's first electric lights, elevators, and swimming pool. It was badly damaged in the devastating 1926 hurricane, and torn down in 1930.

RIGHT: "Approach to Hotel Palm Beach, Palm Beach, Fla." Note the "bicycle buggies," like those in the photograph on page 78.

Baltimore is the logical jumping-off point for a train trip into the great interior of the United States, and not only because it is the head office and terminus of the oldest American railroad. There is a vibrant vein of American popular culture that flows out of the old port city, along with its traditional industrial products, canned oysters, sailcloth, and cigars. That vein ranges from the dark and disturbing to the lighthearted and grotesque, from Edgar Allan Poe, buried here, originally in an unmarked grave, to filmmaker John Waters, a latter-day Baltimore native and resident of the city known variously as Crabtown, Charm City, and Mob Town. Baltimore's writers have chronicled the odd and the picturesque, the obscure and the violent in American culture. Dashiell Hammett, a native Baltimorean, worked as a Pinkerton operative before inventing the hard-boiled detective story. In Hammett's own detective career he once arrested a man for stealing a Ferris wheel from a carnival, only to have the man escape and steal it back from the police impound lot that same night. Baltimore, moreover, though north of the nation's capital, is a profoundly southern city. The state anthem, indeed, refers scathingly to "northern scum."

It is from Baltimore, then, that passengers set out to explore the great American heartland. The train pulls out of Baltimore's Beaux-Arts–style Pennsylvania Station (formerly Union Station) and rolls westward through the lush Maryland countryside along the tracks of the Baltimore and Ohio Railroad, one of the oldest lines in the United States, originally founded in the mid-1820s to compete with New York's Erie Canal as a connection to the rapidly growing interior of the U.S. The B&O was built in the early years of the explosion of railroad construction, and as a result, many of the bridges, overpasses, and tunnels were overengineered in massive neo-Gothic and neo-Romanesque style. Even now, travelers along the B&O (the only one of the four railroads featured in the original Monopoly game that did not run to Atlantic City) will see rough-hewn granite ashlars and finely carved keystones where more recently built railways would feature rusting iron or painted steel.

Rumbling past Antietam, site of one of the bloodiest battles of the Civil War, the line climbs to Martinsburg, West Virginia, where a magnificent old 1866 roundhouse has just been restored. The train then runs through granite-lined gorges to the town of Harpers Ferry, at the confluence of the Shenandoah and

Potomac rivers. The magnificent panorama of sheer cliffs and mighty waters could not have failed to stir late-Romantic souls, but a somber history emanates from the steep little town. It was here that John Brown attempted to seize control of the United States Armory and Arsenal at Harpers Ferry in 1859; he was captured by U.S. troops led by then-Colonel Robert E. Lee. A mighty push toward the bloody Civil War was given here.

As the line tops the Allegheny Mountains, it runs through Cumberland, Maryland. A turn-of-the-century writer described the town: "Cumberland is about 635 feet above sea-level, and from a distance appears to be completely shut in by

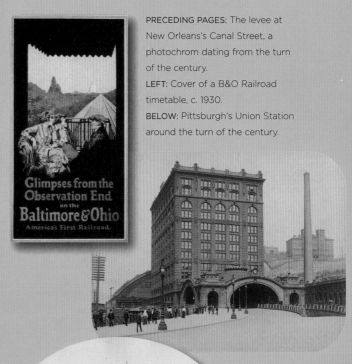

PRECEDING PAGES: The levee at New Orleans's Canal Street, a photochrom dating from the turn of the century.
LEFT: Cover of a B&O Railroad timetable, c. 1930.
BELOW: Pittsburgh's Union Station around the turn of the century.

LEFT: Photochrom of the S.S. *Christopher Columbus* on Lake Michigan. The ship was built in 1893.
BELOW LEFT: Baggage label from the Chittenden Hotel in Columbus, Ohio.

ABOVE: This double-decker streetcar was one of about a dozen built and operated in Pittsburgh. Each seated 110 people.

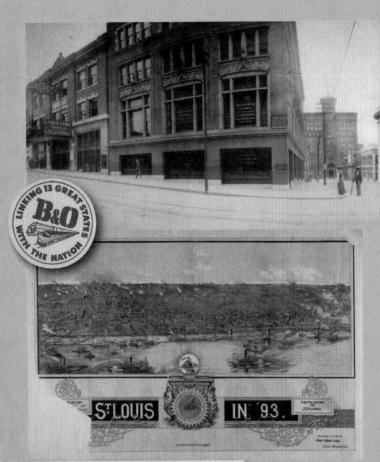

ST. LOUIS IN '93.

ABOVE: Lithograph of St. Louis in 1893. LEFT: This steamboat is making a landing on a river that has clearly flooded its banks, c. 1910.

TOP: This panoramic photograph shows the First National Bank in its brand-new (1906) building at Tenth and Baltimore Street in Kansas City. The building was lavish in its use of marble and mahogany, and the president's office featured a marble fireplace.
RIGHT: When Honest Joe Sater retired as treasurer of Cincinnati in 1877, he was "tendered a complimentary dinner at the St. Nicholas restaurant."
INSETS, ABOVE AND RIGHT: B&O Railroad baggage labels, 1940s.

ST. NICHOLAS
SHELL OYSTERS
RECEIVED DAILY BY EXPRESS.
RESTAURANT
For LADIES & GENTLEMEN,
SOUTH-EAST CORNER OF FOURTH AND RACE STS.
B. ROTH & SONS, Prop'rs.

lofty ranges of hills, which are cut through to the westward by a deep gorge called 'The Narrows,' making a natural gateway of great beauty."

The commanding position of Cumberland was a switching point: from here trains run north to Pittsburgh. As elegant railroad passengers pulled into Pittsburgh in the glory days of American steel making, the dramatic views of river and mountainside gave way to a dramatic series of dioramas, vignettes of black shadow and cascades of sparks, tiny stark figures hauling giant buckets of glowing molten steel: the vast atriums of the steel mills that lined the railroad tracks. Soon, of course, that momentary glimpse of the works gave way to the cool elegance of Pittsburgh's Pennsylvanian Union Station, designed by Daniel Burnham (fully restored in 1987). It is in Pittsburgh, of course, that the rails on which the trains run were physically made.

From here, the traveler can veer north to the Great Lakes. A succession of towns along Ohio's Lake Erie shore are the first to present themselves. Easternmost is Cleveland, once a city of great wealth. Cleveland's Euclid Avenue, inhabited by John D. Rockefeller among others, was known as "Millionaire's Row," and was described as "the most beautiful street in the world." Cleveland owed its wealth to a number of factors: with the construction of the Ohio and Erie Canal, Cleveland stood astride a water connection between the Great Lakes and the Mississippi River; it was also close to Titusville, in northwestern Pennsylvania (and neighboring Oil City, PA), the epicenter of the first oil rush in history.

Westward along the lakeshore lie two more Ohio cities. The first is Sandusky, whose street grid once incorporated a secret Masonic symbol, visible only from the air. The town was a major northern terminus on the Underground Railroad, along which slaves fled the south to freedom in Canada.

Whether the traveler heads due west from here to St. Louis, Missouri, or south, via Memphis and Jackson, to New Orleans, the inevitable destination is the shore of the Mississippi River, the Father of Waters. Those who descended its waters, whether by steamboat or railroad train, had often experienced something similar—in the form of a great painted diorama. John Banvard painted a stretch of the Mississippi River on 1,200 feet of canvas, which was then slowly unrolled for viewers to give the impression of actually sailing past the banks. It was advertised as depicting three miles of the mighty Mississippi. *Yellowstone Science* magazine recently described the experience of viewing a similar panorama: "The moving panorama requires viewers to sit as an audience facing one direction as the painted scenery passes before them in the form of a theatrical backdrop stretched between two rolls of canvas." Henry Lewis's *Mammoth Panorama of the Mississippi River*, 1849, was painted on 45,000 square feet of canvas and toured several cities in the East and Midwest. The unrolling of this painting took several hours, and quasi-scientific commentaries, anecdotal material, and piano music accompanied the images.

All travel along the great Mississippi was only a pale imitation of a glorious and old-fashioned mode of travel— the paddle-wheel steamship. The steamships that ran up and down the Mississippi were sophisticated machines, providing a sophisticated setting. Riverboat gamblers became legendary, but so did the paddle-wheel pilots, legends in their own time. Mark Twain, who was a pilot before he became a successful author, studied every curve, bend, and sandbar in two thousand miles of the great river's course. He was paid well— close to $200,000 in today's money. But he earned as much in experience as he did in cash.

This is Twain's description of a summer sunrise over the Mississippi, from his book *Life on the Mississippi* (1883): "First, there is the eloquence of silence; for a deep hush broods everywhere. Next, there is the haunting sense of loneliness, isolation, remoteness from the worry and bustle of the world. The dawn creeps in stealthily; the solid walls of black forest soften to gray, and vast stretches of the river open up and reveal themselves; the water is glass-smooth, gives off spectral little wreaths of white mist, there is not the faintest breath of wind, nor stir of leaf; the tranquillity is profound and infinitely satis- fying. Then a bird pipes up, another follows, and soon the pipings develop into a jubilant riot of music. You see none of the birds; you simply move through an atmosphere of song which seems to sing itself. When the light has become a little stronger, you have one of the fairest and softest pictures ima- ginable. You have the intense green of the massed and crowded foliage near by; you see it paling shade by shade in front of you; upon the next projecting cape, a mile off or more, the tint has lightened to the tender young green of spring; the cape beyond that one has almost lost color, and the furthest one, miles away under the horizon, sleeps upon the water a mere dim vapor, and hardly separable from the sky above it and about it. And all this stretch of river is a mirror, and you have the shadowy reflections of the leafage and the curving shores and the receding capes pictured in it. Well, that is all beautiful; soft and rich and beautiful; and when the sun gets well up, and distri- butes a pink flush here and a powder of gold yonder and a purple haze where it will yield the best effect, you grant that you have seen something that is worth remembering."

This 1899 lithograph advertising the St. Louis and San Francisco Railroad shows a girl with a doll and a boy with a dog.

As we approached Baltimore, *the waters narrowed and were perfectly calm; we seemed to be going up a river bordered by long avenues. Baltimore offered herself to us as if on the edge of a lake. Opposite the city rose a hill shaded with trees, at the foot of which they were beginning to build a few houses. We tied up at the quay of the port. I slept on board and didn't go ashore until the next day. I went to lodge at the inn where they carried my baggage. . . . Baltimore, like all the other metropolises of the United States, did not have then the extent that it does today. It was a very pretty, clean, and animated city. I paid the captain for my passage and offered him a farewell dinner in a very good tavern near the port. I reserved my seat on the stage that made the trip to Philadelphia three times a week. At four o'clock in the morning I climbed into this stage, and there I was rolling along the highways of the New World, where I knew no one, where I was known to no one at all. My traveling companions had never seen me, and I was never to see them again after our arrival in the capital of Pennsylvania.*

FRANÇOIS-RENÉ CHATEAUBRIAND, 1791

## BALTIMORE

**BOTTOM:** A brochure about "Class A Hotels," offered with the compliments of Baltimore's Belvedere Hotel. The Belvedere was founded in 1903. The morning after its inauguration, the *Baltimore Sun* reported: "The revolving doors on Chase Street were never still. . . . All of the season's debutantes were there."

**OPPOSITE:** The St. Clair Hotel, shown here in a photograph from the 1870s, was a handsome and popular stopping place, clearly modeled with some ambition on the design motif of Venice's Ca' d'Oro. In 1873 and 1874 the National Baseball Association held their annual meetings here. William Makepeace Thackeray stayed here in 1856, when it was known as the Gilmore House. In subsequent years it changed its name to Guy's Monument House, and finally the Imperial Hotel (1881–95).

**ABOVE:** Postcard of Baltimore's Lexington Market, about 1900. It first began purveying fresh foods in 1782, and has been operating on this site ever since. H. L. Mencken, the "Bard of Baltimore," wrote in 1926, "I am glad that I was born long enough ago to remember, now, the days when the town had genuine color, and life here was worth living." The Lexington Market neighborhood epitomizes the Baltimore that Mencken called "this tottering, medieval city."

AFTER A DETESTABLE LUNCHEON, TAKEN AT BALTIMORE IN AN "EATING HOUSE," *I rush off to the station of the Central Pennsylvanian Railway for the West. Thanks to the competition with other lines, one has arrived at the utmost maximum of speed. Thus, at the moment in which I write, and while, according to my wont, I am striving, in spite of horrible shakings, to scribble a few notes in my journal, we are rattling on at a rate of between fifty and sixty miles an hour. . . . The night is beautiful; a full moon floods the whole country with silvery light. As far as the eye can see, the railroad follows a straight line, which enables us to go at a fearful rate during the greater part of the night. A couple of feet below me, all along the sides of the rails, the pebbles and flints, sparkling like diamonds, look like a horizontal cataract. In crossing the trestlework bridge, the train rocks and vacillates like a ship in an angry sea. But I cling to the balustrade, and comfort myself with the reflection that on this line, one of the worst in the States, the greater part of the trains, nevertheless, arrive at their destination.*

BARON DE HÜBNER, 1871

# HARPERS FERRY
# WHITE SULPHUR
# SPRINGS

BOTTOM: The Wistaria [*sic*] Room in the Greenbrier Hotel, White Sulphur Springs, West Virginia, 1910s.
OPPOSITE: This advertisement for the Greenbrier Hotel appeared in the September 1931 issue of *Country Life* magazine. This luxury hotel has been a stopping place for the rich and powerful since its foundation. In the late 1950s the Greenbrier was designated as the emergency location for the government in case of nuclear war.

ABOVE: Harpers Ferry, West Virginia. Thomas Jefferson visited this site in 1783 and called it "perhaps one of the most stupendous scenes in nature." The town occupies the point of land at the confluence of the Potomac and Shenandoah rivers. In 1859 abolitionist John Brown seized control of the United States Armory and Arsenal at Harpers Ferry, only to be captured by a small contingent commanded by U.S. Army Colonel Robert E. Lee, with his aide-de-camp J.E.B. Stuart. This incident triggered the Civil War, and Lee and Stuart were two of the most noted Confederate officers. During the Civil War, Harpers Ferry changed hands thirteen times.

THE ITALIAN GARDEN, BOOK-CADILLAC HOTEL, DETROIT, MICH.

*n, and with a population that was*
*, and which, by a strange blending*
*men and their appliances, and we*
*ented to us, . . . Altogether, it*
*etroit began our surprise at the rapid*
*the setting sun, at a good speed even*
*e villages, of which we must have*
*in size from one to three thousand*
*e excepted. The whole country was*

JAMES FENIMORE COOPER, 1881

PRECEDING PAGES: The *City of Erie*, a 324-foot-long, 78-foot-wide, side-wheel steamer, was the winner of a memorable 100-mile race in the summer of 1901. Racing against the White Star line's *Tashmoo*, the *City of Erie* won by just 45 seconds, at an average speed of 23 miles per hour. The few passengers allowed on board during the race were confined to their cabins, lest even a few figures on deck create wind resistance.

OPPOSITE: A 1901 photochrom of Cleveland's Arcade. Built in 1888, the Arcade consists of two nine-story office buildings linked halfway up by an enormous iron-and-glass "sky light" roof.

ABOVE LEFT: Detroit's Woodward Avenue in 1925; note the billboard on the right: "Every woman can now afford to wear silk. Underwear, gloves, hosiery."

ABOVE RIGHT: Postcard of daily river excursions, Detroit. Note the *Tashmoo*, in the foreground, which raced against the *City of Erie*.

LEFT: The Book-Cadillac Hotel, one of Detroit's luxurious stopping places, abandoned for twenty years in the depth of the city's financial crisis, and newly renovated in 2008.

OVERLEAF: Detroit skyline along Lake Erie in 1929, as seen from the Canadian lakeshore.

FACSIMILE: Postcard of the Italian Garden in the Book-Cadillac Hotel, postmarked January 20, 1930.

On the two overwarm afternoons we hiked out on the massive Grand Sable Dunes *having discovered that the insects were averse to this sandy terrain. It was hard walking but there were shaded sandbanks of blooming wild sweet pea and sea rose, and wild strawberries which we'd eat despite the sand embedded in them. On the highest edges of the dunes you could sit and simply stare down at the icy clarity of Lake Superior, or look far out to sea and note passing ore freighters.*

Jim Harrison, 1960s

13899 OFF FOR THE UPPER LAKES.

## SAULT STE. MARIE
## LAKE SUPERIOR

OPPOSITE, TOP: The whaleback steamer *Joseph L. Colby* leaves the Poe lock (one of the Sault Locks, usually called the "Soo" Locks) in Sault Ste. Marie, Michigan (1891). The whaleback steamer was invented by Captain Alexander McDougall in the 1880s. The idea was to build a covered steel boat that would keep ore and grain shipments dry in the brutal Great Lakes winter storms. Capt. McDougall even shot the St. Lawrence rapids in one of the whaleback barges and sailed it to Liverpool.

OPPOSITE, BOTTOM: Turn-of-the-century postcard, captioned "Off for the Upper Lakes."

ABOVE: Stella Cove, in Wisconsin's Lake Superior Apostle Islands. These islands were once inhabited and are now a national lakeshore park. Many ships were wrecked in lake storms along these rocky coasts.

LEFT: Chippewa Indians fishing in the St. Mary's Rapids at Sault Ste. Marie, on Lake Superior, in 1901. Note the 1888 International Railroad Bridge in the distance.

I FIND MYSELF IN A GREAT AVENUE *on the banks of the lake, with a row of magnificent buildings on the other side. This is the celebrated Michigan Avenue, the quarter of the plutocracy of Chicago. In these splendid mansions, all of wood, but plastered over, and built in every imaginable style, Italian, Classic, Gothic, Roman. or Elizabethan, each and all surrounded by pretty gardens bright with flowers, live the families of men who, in a few years, have realized millions. . . . I have been walking for more than an hour, and I am not yet at the end of this street. You might fancy yourself in the country. None but women and children are to be seen, with a few private carriages, and no omnibuses. There is an air of rest and idleness over the whole. Babies play in the little gardens, ladies, elegantly dressed, lie on the verandas, and rock themselves in armchairs, holding in one hand a fan, and in the other a novel.*

BARON DE HÜBNER, 1871

## CHICAGO

PRECEDING PAGES: A steamboat passing under Chicago's 12th Street bascule drawbridge just after the turn of the century. Note the advertisement for daily excursions to the "drainage canal." In 1900 Chicago built a canal and reversed the flow of the Chicago River; until that project was complete, the city's sewage had been flowing into Lake Michigan, the source of Chicago's drinking water. The Chicago Sanitary and Ship Canal was recently named a "Civil Engineering Monument of the Millennium."

OPPOSITE: Randolph Street, looking east from LaSalle. Note Powers' Theatre on the left, one of Chicago's great historical stages.

ABOVE LEFT: Cover of a commemorative booklet, comparing the Chicago lakefront in 1831 and a century later.

ABOVE RIGHT: Turn-of-the-century zoo-goers watching a black bear climb a tree in Chicago's Lincoln Park.

LEFT: Postcard of Grant Park and Michigan Avenue. Note the Blackstone Hotel on the left, a venerable "Hotel of Presidents."

OVERLEAF: The Lake Michigan beachfront and the Drake Hotel, newly opened in 1920.

I HAVE NOT OFTEN SEEN A PLACE THAT COMMENDS ITSELF SO FAVOURABLY AND PLEASANTLY TO A STRANGER *at the first glance as this does: with its clean houses of red and white, its well-paved roads, and foot-ways of bright tile. Nor does it become less prepossessing on a closer acquaintance. The streets are broad and airy, the shops extremely good, the private residences remarkable for their elegance and neatness. There is something of invention and fancy in the varying styles of these latter erections, which, after the dull company of the steamboat, is perfectly delightful, as conveying an assurance that there are such qualities still in existence. The disposition to ornament these pretty villas and render them attractive, leads to the culture of trees and flowers, and the laying out of well-kept gardens, the sight of which, to those who walk along the streets, is inexpressibly refreshing and agreeable. I was quite charmed with the appearance of the town, and its adjoining suburb of Mount Auburn: from which the city, lying in an amphitheatre of hills, forms a picture of remarkable beauty, and is seen to great advantage.*

CHARLES DICKENS, 1842

## CINCINNATI

ABOVE: The Ohio River in Cincinnati, 1911, with the John A. Roebling Suspension Bridge in the background. Completed in 1866, the bridge was a forerunner of the Brooklyn Bridge, which Roebling designed and his son completed.
RIGHT: An 1894 poster advertising Pullman car service on the Cincinnati, Hamilton & Dayton Railroad. It is not only an eloquent document on the social system of the period but also rich in advertising history. Note the number of advertising "plugs": Peebles Whisky and Cigars being brought in by the porter, a bottle of Aurora Export beer on the table, a Cook Carriage Co. poster on the floor, a Mosler Safe factory outside the window, and Wing Shot gunpowder in the parcel rack above the window. The poster was printed in the midst of the Panic of 1893, just months before the dramatic Pullman Strike of 1894.
OPPOSITE: The 24-hour-a-day Colonial Kitchen in Cincinnati's Alms Hotel, "a city within a city," as an ad of the time (1930s) called it. The hotel had 300 employees and as many as 3,000 guests.

# LOUISVILLE

ABOVE: The Seelbach Hotel in Louisville, Kentucky, was a paragon of elegance in the early part of the twentieth century. In *The Great Gatsby*, Scott Fitzgerald describes the wedding of Tom and Daisy Buchanan: "She married Tom Buchanan of Chicago, with more pomp and circumstance than Louisville ever knew before. He came down with a hundred people in four private cars, and hired a whole floor of the Seelbach Hotel, and the day before the wedding he gave her a string of pearls valued at three hundred and fifty thousand dollars."

FAR LEFT: An 1868 label from a package of Pioneer Tobacco. Tobacco was Kentucky's largest cash crop for many years, a mainstay of the state's economy, and the hunter in the drawing is wearing the coonskin cap traditionally identified with Daniel Boone, who explored and settled Kentucky.

LEFT: The Seelbach Hotel in its glory years, the 1920s. The neoclassical hotel was built in 1903–5 by Bavarian-born brothers Louis and Otto Seelbach and featured, among other attractions, a spectacular German-style rathskeller, covered with Rookwood pottery. The ceilings are upholstered in fine-tooled leather.

RIGHT: A view of Louisville's White City, an early amusement park built in 1907 on the banks of the Ohio River. The ride shown is a roller coaster that plunged riders into a pool of water with a spectacular splash—a pioneering and novel approach at the time.

After a day of close and intense September heat, *it had rained during the night. And now the morning had followed chill and crisp, yet with possibilities of a genial sunshine breaking through the mist that had risen at dawn from the great sluggish river and spread itself through the mazes of the city. . . . The St. Louis Exposition was in progress with all its many allurements that had been heralded for months through the journals of the State. Hence, the unusual press of people on the streets this bright September morning. Home people, whose air of ownership to the surroundings classified them at once, moving unobservantly about their affairs. Women and children from the near and rich country towns, in for the Exposition and their fall shopping; wearing gowns of ultra fashionable tendencies; . . . There were whole families from across the bridge, hurrying towards the Exposition.*

Kate Chopin, 1890

# ST. LOUIS

ABOVE: The Eads Bridge, across the Mississippi River, was completed in 1874, as shown in this Currier & Ives print. An engineering marvel of the time, the bridge cost $10 million and was—still is, actually—over a mile long. Crossing it must have been one of the signal experiences of any transcontinental train trip.

LEFT: The 1904 Louisiana Purchase Exposition, better known as the St. Louis World's Fair, commemorated the centennial of the French sale of 828,000 sq. miles (2,140,000 sq. km) of land to the administration of Thomas Jefferson (the sale actually took place in 1803). It was the central event in the lives of a St. Louis family in the Vincente Minelli film *Meet Me in St. Louis,* starring Judy Garland.

OPPOSITE: An ad from the mid-1950s for the new Boulevard Room in the Jefferson Hotel, St. Louis. Built in time for the 1904 World's Fair, the Jefferson was sold to the Sheraton chain in 1955.

OVERLEAF: Photographer Lewis Hine traveled the country documenting child labor in the early decades of the twentieth century. This 1916 photograph was of Maurice Livingston, who worked for the Southern Express Co.

WE WERE ABOUT TO ENTER UPON THAT VAST ELEVATED REGION *which forms the southern division of the Appalachian mountain system, and constitutes the culminating point in the Atlantic barrier of the American continent. We stood at the gate of the lands through which runs the chain of the Iron, Smoky, and Unaka mountains, separating North Carolina from Eastern Tennessee. Beyond the blue line of hills faintly discerned in the rainy twilight from the windows of our little room lay the grand table-land, two thousand feet above the heated air of cities and the contagion of civilization; and there a score of mountain peaks reached up six thousand feet into the crystal atmosphere; torrents ran impetuously down their steep sides into noble valleys; there was the solitude of the cañon, the charm of the dizzy climb along the precipice brink, the shade of the forests where no woodman's axe had yet profaned the thickets. . . . This day's journey was but a succession of grand panoramic views of gorge and height. Descending, we rode for several miles along a path cut out of the mountain's steep side; and hundreds of feet below us saw the tops of tall pines and spruces. Not a human habitation was to be seen; there was no sign of life save when a ruffled grouse or a rabbit sprang across the track.*

EDWARD KING, 1874

116

GREAT SMOKY MOUNTAINS
HOT SPRINGS

OPPOSITE: The Little River Gorge is a steep section of what is now the Great Smoky Mountains National Park. In 1909 the Little River Lumber Company purchased a new Baldwin 2-4-4-2 locomotive: no. 148. It hauled heavy lumber cars up the grade during the week, and on weekends it hauled heavyweight passenger cars on excursions through the beautiful mountain landscape.

ABOVE: The Arlington Hotel, seen at the turn of the century, is a 500-room hotel in the spa town of Hot Springs, Arkansas. In the 1930s it was a favorite stopping place of Al Capone. Hot Springs' Bathhouse Row is a tourist attraction, as is Oaklawn Racetrack.

RIGHT: In the early 20th century, Hot Springs also featured an Ostrich Farm, where it was possible to ride in a cart pulled by an ostrich. The farm had over 200 ostriches, and the owner regularly raced his birds against horses.

THE TITLE TO A WELL KNOWN WATERING PLACE IN THE STATE OF ARKANSAS, *called the Hot Springs, now located in Hot Springs County, has been contested by a number of claimants for nearly half a century. These springs are situated in a narrow valley or ravine between two rocky ridges in one of the lateral ranges of the Ozark Mountains, about sixty miles to the westward of Little Rock. Though not easily accessible, and in a district of country claimed by the Indians until after the Treaty made with the Quapaws in 1818, they were considerably frequented by invalids and others as early as 1810 or 1812; but no permanent settlement was made at the place until a number of years afterwards. Temporary cabins were erected by visitors, . . . but were only occupied during a portion of the year. The public surveys were not extended to that portion of the country until 1838. . . . In conclusion, we feel bound to decide that none of the claimants are entitled to the lands in question.*

SUPREME COURT JUSTICE JOSEPH P. BRADLEY, 1876

## HOT SPRINGS
## LITTLE ROCK

TOP: Panoramic view of Hot Springs, Arkansas. The building at right is the Eastman Hotel. In March 1912 the *New York Times* reported that Hot Springs was "experiencing the banner season in its history." The paper noted that railroad baron Jay Gould's son Frank stayed ten days at the Eastman before setting out on an "extensive Southern tour in Mr. Gould's private [railroad] car."

ABOVE  Markham Street in Little Rock, Arkansas's capital.
OPPOSITE: Vintage postcards from Hot Springs.

OVERLEAF: This 1895 heliotype print depicts the various forms of commerce along the Mississippi River, whose basin appears in the map on the upper left. Steamboats plied the river until the 1930s, and the largest delivery of cotton ever made by steamboat reached New Orleans in 1930 (eight barges with 30,000 bales). Cotton is the other great protagonist of this print: bolls at the center bottom, bales aboard the steamboat, and a plantation in the background. Note the raft: in 1895 the largest lumber raft ever floated reached St. Louis. It contained 600 train carloads of pine. Also, note the steam organ in the lower left corner.

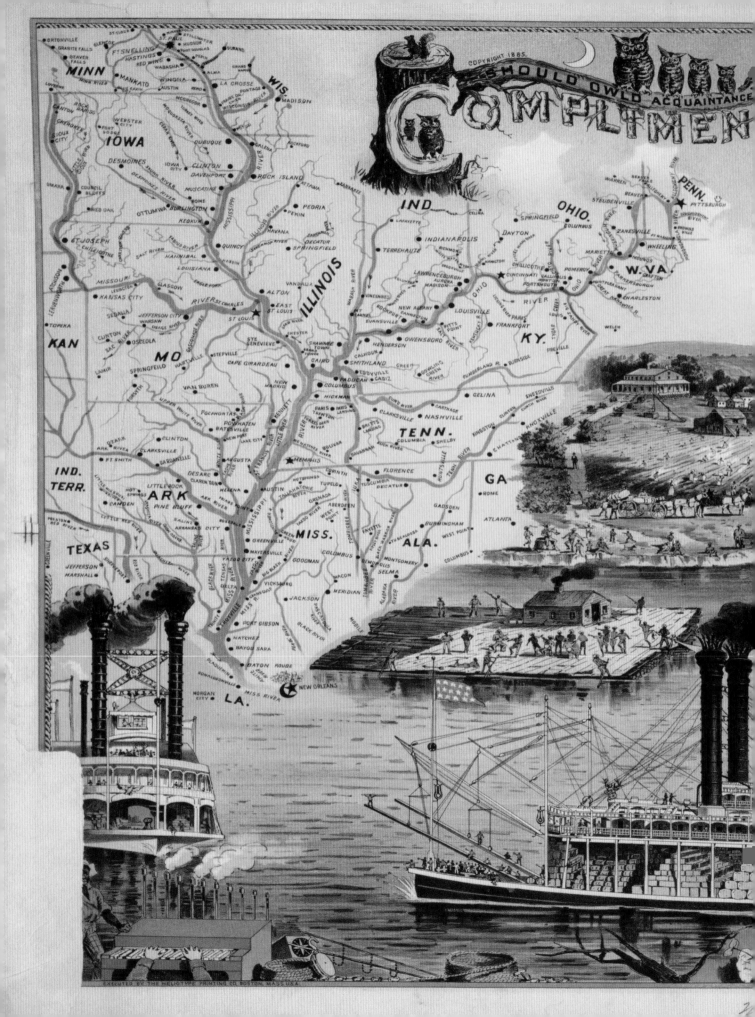

ississippi River Steamboat

*New Orleans was such a strange, glamorous place and Scarlett enjoyed it with the headlong pleasure of a pardoned life prisoner. . . . The people she met seemed to have all the money they wanted and no cares at all. Rhett introduced her to dozens of women, pretty women in bright gowns, women who had soft hands that showed no signs of hard work, women who laughed at everything and never talked of stupid serious things or hard times. And the men she met—how thrilling they were! And how different from Atlanta men—and how they fought to dance with her, and paid her the most extravagant compliments as though she were a young belle. These men had the same hard reckless look Rhett wore. . . . Sometimes when Rhett was alone with them and Scarlett in the next room, she heard laughter and caught fragments of conversation that meant nothing to her, scraps of words, puzzling names—Cuba and Nassau in the blockade days, the gold rush and claim jumping, gun running and filibustering, Nicaragua and William Walker and how he died against a wall at Truxillo. Once her sudden entrance abruptly terminated a conversation about what had happened to the members of Quantrill's band of guerillas, and she caught the names of Frank and Jesse James. But they were all well mannered, beautifully tailored, and they evidently admired her, so it mattered little to Scarlett that they chose to live utterly in the present.*

MARGARET MITCHELL, 1936

## NEW ORLEANS

**TOP:** The Roosevelt Hotel, currently known as the Fairmont, in New Orleans in the 1940s. The hotel was originally known as the Grunewald when it opened in 1893.
**BOTTOM:** The Cave Restaurant in the Grunewald Hotel is thought to have been America's first nightclub. It featured "waterfalls, stalactites, and chorus girls dancing to Dixieland jazz." The hotel was built by a German immigrant, Louis Grunewald, and so the "cave" motif may have been a reference to the German rathskeller tradition.
**OPPOSITE:** A menu from the St. Charles Hotel, dated January 3, 1857. Lady Emmeline Stuart-Wortley called the St. Charles hotel "the finest piece of architecture she had seen anywhere in the New World," and compared its dome to that of St. Peter's in Rome.
**OVERLEAF:** The French Quarter in New Orleans in the 1870s. Note the wrought-iron balconies.

# ST. CHARLES

## TABLE D'HOTE.

### New Orleans, Saturday, Jan. 3, 1857.

### Gentlemen's Ordinary.

#### SOUPS.

Oyster gombo | Macaroni

#### FISH

Baked Redfish, port wine sauce

#### BOILED.

Corned Beef and Cabbage | Leg of Mutton, with capers | Bacon and greens
Fulton Market beef | Chicken and pork

Cold roast beef | Cold Fulton | Cold beef tongue
Market Corned Beef

Crabs stuffed and baked
Bread of fat livers with jelly
Stewed mutton with onions and potatoes
Fried oysters
Chicken pot-pie family style
Round of beef, à la mode

#### ENTREES.

Canards aux olives
Poîtrine de mouton glacé, aux épinards
Ailerons de dindon, au celeri
Ris de veau, à la Valencienne
Fricandeau sauce tomate
Foie de volaille sauté, aux champignons
Macaroni au gratin
Blanquette de veau, aux navets

#### VEGETABLES

Potatoes boiled, fried baked, and mashed | Sweet potatoes baked

New potatoes | Rice | Beets | Hominy | Spinage
Turnips | Lettuce | Onions | Carrots

#### ROAST.

Beef | Saddle of mutton | Chicken | Turkey
Pork | Veal

#### SECOND COURSE.

Mallard ducks

#### PASTRY

Bread and butter pudding | Currant tarts
Orange pies | Genoises
Gooseberry pies | Swiss meringue

#### DESSERT.

Pecans | Almonds | | Prunes
Bananas | Apples | Raisins | Oranges

Picayune Print, 66 Camp street.

## HALL & HILDRETH

# NEW ORLEANS

**ABOVE:** Turn-of-the-century photo-chrom of Royal Street in New Orleans, one of the oldest streets in the city, in one of its oldest neighborhoods, the French Quarter. New Orleans, and the entire Louisiana Purchase (extending north along the course of the Mississippi and covering most of the center of what is now the United States) were originally French possessions.

**LEFT:** Note the numerous stereotypes in this lithograph of a "plantation banjo player," including the foolish smile and the jug of whiskey concealed behind the chair.

**RIGHT:** A 1905 photochrom of "coons in a cotton shed," another ethnic slur; note the interesting inclusion of a white ragamuffin on the left.

**OPPOSITE:** Another turn-of-the-century photochrom of the French Market in New Orleans. This is one of the oldest sections of the city, dating back to the 1790s, and has been a popular tourist attraction for almost that long.

**OVERLEAF:** Oyster smacks pulled up along the levee around 1900.
**OVERLEAF, FACSIMILE:** a folder of ready-to-mail souvenir postcards of New Orleans, 1919.

On a bright afternoon *they would gather in their gay, picturesque finery, by hundreds, even thousands, under the shade of the sycamores, to dance the Bamboula or the Calinda; the music of their Creole songs tuned by the beating of the tam-tam. "Dansez Calinda! Badoum! Badoum!" the children, dancing too on the outskirts, adding their screams and romping to the chorus and movement. A bazaar of refreshments filled the sidewalks around; lemonade, ginger beer, pies, and the ginger cakes called "estomac mulattre," set out on deal tables, screened with cotton awnings, whose variegated streamers danced also in the breeze. . . . A word, "Voudou," changes the gay, careless Sunday scene into its diabolic counterpart, a witches' sabbat, the evening to midnight, the open square to hidden obscure corners, the dancers to bacchanals; the gay, frank music to a weird chanting, subtly imitative of the yearning sighing of the wind that precedes the tropical storm; rising and swelling to the full explosion of the tempest.*

Grace Elizabeth King, 1896

Romantic City Park.

HE LA

Made by Curt Teich & Co., Chicago, Ill.

ONE OF THE MOST CHARMING MEMORIES OF MY OWN HAPPY YEARS IN BILOXI, *on the Gulf coast, was the visit of a week from Judge and Mrs. Gayarré. It was in the time of roses and jasmine, and the famed mocking-birds of the coast woke us to enjoy the moonlight on the sea, and to listen to that mysterious music under the water which has so attracted the attention of men of science and become the source of legend and poetry. We walked the shell-strewn ways under the live oaks; we drove under the pines, and knelt together in the parish church, which, not far distant from Beauvoir, was the place of worship of the late Jefferson Davis and his family, and, when quarantine regulations permitted, that of the officers of the Government stationed at Ship Island and the Chandeleurs. Biloxi is the summer home of many New Orleans and Mobile families, and a resort of winter tourists. Its local traditions as we lingered over our morning chocolate gained new value from Gayarré's reminiscences, vivid as that dramatic chapter, "The Battle of Roncal," in which he has portrayed the sons and lions of Navarre following to the rescue of their chief.*

LAURA F. HINSDALE, 1890

# BILOXI

OPPOSITE: Old oak tree at the Shady Oaks Hotel, Biloxi, Mississippi, in a turn-of-the-century photochrom. The Shady Oaks later became the Montross, and later still the Riviera. Biloxi was a destination in part because it was healthier than the swampy interior.

TOP LEFT AND BOTTOM RIGHT: Southern Pacific carfloat *Mastodon*, crossing the Mississippi River at Avondale, Louisiana, ten miles north of New Orleans. The largest in the world when it was built in 1909, it carried almost thirty freight cars. One of the other carfloats operating at Avondale was the *El Grande*, seen here in 1900.

TOP RIGHT: Photochrom of the Biloxi Light in 1901. Built in 1848, it was automated in 1941. During its long life, this lighthouse on the Gulf of Mexico was kept by more female lighthouse keepers than any other lighthouse in the United States.

In 1903 there were no gas stations in the United States. The country had barely a hundred miles of paved road—and none of that was outside the cities. The golden era of train travel was just subsiding, as was the bicycle craze that had swept the country in the 1880s and 1890s. The Wright Brothers had a successful bicycle business; as a pioneering sideline, they developed the first self-propelled heavier-than-air flying machine.

In those same venturesome years, a Vermont physician with the heroic, if improbable, name of Horatio Nelson Jackson, bet fifty dollars that he could drive from San Francisco to New York in just three months. Driving a slightly used Winton touring car, Jackson made the trip in sixty-four days, and encountered all sorts of relics of an earlier age, including pioneers heading west in covered wagons, and cowboys with lariats who kindly pulled his car out of sand drifts.

This was the first cross-country American road trip. In the eastern section of the country, the focus had been on train travel, but cars began to crisscross the continent surprisingly early. Indeed, the introduction of the automobile into American life took the form of long-distance travel almost immediately. What came later was the car in the cities: trolleys ran everywhere, and the streets were often too narrow to allow for much parking.

In the first half of the century, the American road trip morphed from exciting adventure to the family outing documented in Normal Rockwell's classic diptych *Going and Coming* (1947). While Rockwell's subjects are often folksy, he was a sly social commentator—born and raised in Manhattan and classically trained. *Going and Coming* is a pair of paintings (the cover of an August issue of the *Saturday Evening Post*) that tell a sly joke about car travel and vacationing. In *Going* a family sets out for a holiday by car. The father puffs cheerfully on a cigar in the morning light, the four children and the dog are boisterous and excited. *Coming* shows the return home. Night is falling, a streetlamp glows in the background. The father hunches over the steering wheel; the dog is tired, the children subdued.

The love of dramatic scenery and extended automobile and railroad trips—travel across the newer, westernmost United States was nothing if not time-consuming—has its origin in the Romantic love of stark contrast. Before the Romantics, mountains and canyons were bad things, as Leslie Stephen, father of Virginia Woolf, pointed out in 1871. Referring to a guidebook in his personal library that was published in 1713, Stephen notes

PRECEDING PAGES: Photochrom of Bright Angel Canyon as seen from O'Neill's Point, about 1900.
RIGHT: A Works Project Administration poster advertising the Grand Canyon National Park in 1938 as a "free government service."
BELOW: "The Dawn of Day," a 1915 photograph of a Navajo man on horseback as the sun rises behind a butte.

A FREE GOVERNMENT SERVICE
GRAND CANYON
NATIONAL PARK
U.S. DEPARTMENT OF THE INTERIOR
NATIONAL PARK SERVICE

ABOVE: This photochrom of the Georgetown Loop Railroad features the Devil's Gate Bridge in Clear Creek Canyon, Colorado, not far from Denver.

RIGHT: A cowboy in French author Huret's book *Amerique Moderne*, 1911.

ABOVE: Harvey's Casa del Desierto, in Barstow, California, around 1911.
LEFT: Family of four purchasing gas around 1920 at a Conoco service station.

The Harvey House chain ultimately included nearly a hundred hotels, and a list of those hotels takes us back to a time of gracious yet efficient living. The Harvey restaurants had developed a set of signals that allowed them to feed an entire trainload of travelers on fine china with elegant Irish linen in just thirty minutes.

In 1883 Fred Harvey decided to replace his rowdy male staff with single, well-mannered, and educated waitresses. The girls worked under strict supervision, with an early curfew, and wore an official starched black-and-white uniform. The mythology of the period claims that the Harvey girls helped "civilize the American Southwest." And that legend found its way into film, in the 1946 MGM musical *The Harvey Girls*. It starred Judy Garland and introduced the Johnny Mercer/Harry Warren classic "On the Atchison, Topeka and the Santa Fe."

The Harvey Houses were conceived for train travel, but they continued to serve motorists on the great transcontinental highways: 6, 50 (The Lincoln Highway), and 66. The drive across country turned into a sensual experience—visual, but also aural and olfactory. Journalist and author Roger Angell recalled the joys of the early-twentieth-century road trips in a 2003 *New Yorker* article. Angell was eighty-three when he wrote the article "Romance," subtitled: "Car trips in the nineteen-thirties took you to some unexpected places."

"Every family has its own car stories," he wrote, "but in another sense we know them all in advance now, regardless of our age. The collective American unconscious is stuffed with old Pontiacs." His article is filled with vivid memories of road trips from seventy years ago: "Car travel was bumpier and curvier back then, with more traffic lights and billboards, more cows and hillside graveyards, no air-conditioning and almost no interstates, and with tin cans and Nehi signs and red Burma-Shave jingles crowding the narrow roadside."

Burma-Shave was a brushless shaving cream (an innovation at the time) that advertised with successions of rhyming roadside billboards. The humor was folksy and focused on the brand-new hazards and pitfalls of driving: "Don't stick / Your elbow / Out so far / It might go home / In another car / Burma Shave."

Angell brilliantly evokes the smells of driving, in the days when the only source of cool air was an open window: "the hot, flat scent of tall corn; a sudden tang of skunk come and gone; the smell of tar when the dirt roads stopped, fainter now with

that it claimed God could not have been entirely wrong when he created mountains. Mountains are "useful as sending down rivers to the sea" and "they are an excellent preserve for fur-bearing animals." Stephen goes on to say that a century before he was writing, people clearly "hated the mountains as a seasick traveler hates the ocean, though he may feebly remind himself that it is a good place for the fish."

As the great western expanses of the United States opened up to tourism, the Romantic ideals of grandeur and nature began to trickle down to the general public. And that general public ventured out west, lured by the paintings of Albert Bierstadt and other artists of the magnificent western landscape. They went dressed in formal clothing, so that when we look at old photographs of women and girls in floor-length skirts and elegant hats, and men and boys in formal suits with tie and top hat or bowler in the middle of the desert, we are perplexed about just where they thought they were. But while lightweight, high-tech hiking gear is an advantage we may enjoy, they may very well have seen the spectacular landscape with fresher, more astonishable eyes than we possess today.

There is one realm, though, in which we can only envy our forebears, and that is the hotels that they frequented. And one of the forgotten geniuses behind those western hotels was Fred Harvey. He built a chain of close to fifty Harvey House restaurants and fifteen magnificent hotels spanning the American Southwest, and he ran thirty railroad cars on the Santa Fe Railway. His dying words to the sons who inherited his empire were: "Don't cut the ham too thin, boys."

the hot sun gone; and, over a rare pond or creek as the tire noise went deeper, something rich and dank, with cowflop and dead fish mixing with the sweet-water weeds."

A movie that first evoked our current road-trip nostalgia was Peter Bogdanovich's 1973 masterpiece, *Paper Moon*. Starring Ryan O'Neal and his eight-year-old daughter, Tatum, the movie evoked the American highways of the Great Depression, especially the Great Plains region. Made in black and white, it features flim-flam artists, rural yokels, and small-town Valentinos—and roads of all kinds: dirt, gravel, and paved.

Many of these highway routes paralleled the cross-country railroad lines. The United States at the turn of the century boasted a number of prestigious luxury passenger lines. Foremost among them was the Twentieth Century Limited, which ran from Chicago to New York but became emblematic of deluxe rail travel. The line was founded in 1902 by a patent medicine salesman turned passenger agent. By 1932 the name Twentieth Century also described a hit Broadway play written by Ben Hecht and Charles MacArthur, and a new motion picture studio. In 1934 it was a wildly popular film starring Carole Lombard and John Barrymore.

Other famous rail lines crossing the country included the Super Chief (Train of the Stars), the City of Los Angeles, and the Golden State. All three ran from Los Angeles to Chicago. And all three were bastions of luxury in the western half of the country.

But one roadside attraction in particular can stand in for them all—the Corn Palace in Mitchell, South Dakota. First constructed in 1892, the Corn Palace—like many other attractions in the Great Plains—was intended to attract farmers. It is a multipurpose structure, big enough to hold conventions and basketball games, and it is decorated with corn, nailed to the exterior walls painstakingly, ear by ear, along with other grains and native grasses to form murals that change every summer. Half a million people visit the Corn Palace every year, and the corn murals have been presented annually for over a century. The building features minarets and kiosks of Moorish design.

It is one of a thousand different roadside attractions. If the carnival and the circus once "came to town," by the time the American family was regularly crisscrossing the country in an era of cheap gas, paved highways, and trailer camps, the circus only needed to pitch its tent by the side of the highway.

LEFT: The Corn Palace in Mitchell, South Dakota, c. 1909.
BELOW: A crossroads grocery store, bar, juke joint, and gas station, c. 1940. The emphasis on alcohol might be less marked in a modern-day American roadside attraction.

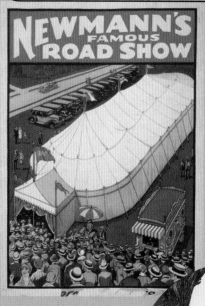

LEFT: This color lithograph for "Newmann's Famous Road Show," 1925, advertised the magic and hypnotism of Christian Andrew George Naeseth, known as Newmann the Great, or C. A. George Newmann. He toured the Northwest and West Coast with a show of hypnotism, mentalism, and "fun and wonders."

INSET: Commemorative Route 66 decal.

ONE OF MY MOST VIVID MEMORIES *is of coming back west from prep school and later from college at Christmas time. Those who went farther than Chicago would gather in the old dim Union Station. . . . I remember the fur coats of the girls . . . and the chatter of frozen breath . . . and the long green tickets clasped tight in our gloved hands. And last the murky yellow cars of the Chicago, Milwaukee and St. Paul Railroad looking cheerful as Christmas itself on the tracks beside the gate. When we pulled out into the winter night and the real snow, our snow, began to stretch out beside us and twinkle against the windows, and the dim lights of small Wisconsin stations moved by, a sharp wild brace came suddenly into the air. We drew in deep breaths of it as we walked back from dinner through the cold vestibules, unutterably aware of our identity with this country for one strange hour before we melted indistinguishably into it again. That's my middle west—. . . the thrilling, returning trains of my youth and the street lamps and sleigh bells in the frosty dark and the shadows of holly wreaths thrown by lighted windows on the snow.*

F. SCOTT FITZGERALD, 1925

## CHICAGO

OPPOSITE: This photograph of the Union Station waiting room was taken in February 1943 by Jack Delano, who traveled the country in the early 1940s for the federal Farm Security Administration. Photographers Walker Evans, Dorothea Lange, and Gordon Parks were also working for the FSA at that time. Note the dramatic effect of the low February sunlight.

ABOVE: Baggage label from 1940, proclaiming the City of Denver as the "world's fastest long distance train." Service began in 1936.

ABOVE: In March 1943 Jack Delano took this picture of a freight train about to leave for the west coast from the Santa Fe Corwith Rail Yards in Chicago. Note the Grand Canyon Line boxcar.

RIGHT: The Union Station concourse was completed in the 1920s, part of a new structure that cost $65 million. Sadly, the concourse was demolished in 1969.

ST. PAUL? . . . *I don't know of any lovelier view than when you stand on Summit Avenue and look across Lower Town to the Mississippi cliffs and the upland farms beyond. . . . They walked from St. Paul down the river to Mendota. . . . The High Bridge crosses the Mississippi, mounting from low banks to a palisade of cliffs. Far down beneath it on the St. Paul side, upon mud flats, is a wild settlement of chicken-infested gardens and shanties patched together from discarded sign-boards, sheets of corrugated iron, and planks fished out of the river. Carol leaned over the rail of the bridge to look down at this Yang-tse village. . . . From the cliffs across the river Carol and Kennicott looked back at St. Paul on its hills; an imperial sweep from the dome of the cathedral to the dome of the state capitol. The river road led past rocky field slopes, deep glens, woods flamboyant now with September, to Mendota, white walls and a spire among trees beneath a hill, old-world in its placid ease. And for this fresh land, the place is ancient.*

SINCLAIR LEWIS, 1920

OMAHA
MINNEAPOLIS
ST. PAUL

ABOVE: This silver gelatin photograph of the staff of the Omaha Merchant's Express and Transfer Company was taken in 1908 by Frederick J. Bandholtz, a traveling photographer. Bandholtz was in Iowa in 1907, and took a panoramic shot of Deadwood, South Dakota, in 1909.

TOP RIGHT: Baggage label from the Hiawatha "Speedliner" Service of the Milwaukee Railroad. The slogan put the accent on speed: "Nothing faster on rails."

BOTTOM RIGHT: This 1880 print of the University of Minnesota at Minneapolis features various activities, including military drill exercises. Neither of the buildings shown still exists. The oldest existing building on the Minneapolis campus, Eddy Hall, dates from 1886.

OPPOSITE: The Ryan Hotel in Minneapolis's sister city, St. Paul, was built by Denis Ryan after he struck it rich prospecting for gold in Montana. It opened in 1885. This 1924 black-and-white print shows the hotel as it was rebuilt following a devastating fire in 1897. It was demolished in 1962 and replaced by a parking lot.

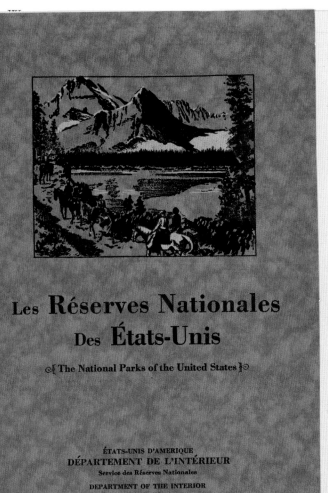

Les **Réserves Nationales** Des **États-Unis**

❦{ The National Parks of the United States }❧

ÉTATS-UNIS D'AMÉRIQUE
**DÉPARTEMENT DE L'INTÉRIEUR**
Service des Réserves Nationales

**DEPARTMENT OF THE INTERIOR**
National Park Service

oTTom, *it broke short off into steep bluffs, up which none but a*
*ahead; just as he turned off the ledge, and as I was right*
*sand bluff, overbalanced itself, and, after standing erect on its*
*pause while it stood bolt upright, gave me time to make a frantic*
*me, and we both clung with hands and hoofs to the side of the*
*ults as I ever saw, and landed with a crash at the bottom of the*
*ot a bit. After a moment or two it struggled to its legs, shook itself,*
*not in the least the worse for the fall.*

THEODORE ROOSEVELT, 1885

PRECEDING PAGES: This photograph of a short Burlington & Missouri River in Nebraska Railroad train (loco-motive, tender, mail car, and one passenger car) stopped in a cutting was taken near Hot Springs, South Dakota, in 1891 by prolific western photographer John C. H. Grabill.

OPPOSITE: This 1901 photochrom is entitled "In the Vale of Minne-kah-ta." Minnekahta is the original Indian name for Hot Springs, *kahta* meaning "hot," and *minne* meaning "water" (as in Minnesota and Minneapolis). Minnekahta is still the name of the larger valley in which Hot Springs is located. It became especially popular in the wake of the South Dakota gold rush that made the Black Hills town of Deadwood (about fifty miles away) so famous.

ABOVE LEFT: Tourists from Sioux City en route to the Great Hot Springs of Dakota, 1889. The long dress of one of the women seated atop the stage partly conceals the inscription "Tally-Ho Coach," which describes a conveyance drawn by four horses.

ABOVE RIGHT: Workmen on the face of George Washington at Mt. Rushmore, in South Dakota. Amazingly, in the course of the famous carving of the four American presidents, there were injuries, but no deaths. The project was authorized by President Calvin Coolidge (a Republican), who insisted that alongside Washington there be two Republicans and a Democrat. The project was meant as a way of promoting tourism in the area.

FACSIMILE: A United States National Parks brochure in French, 1931.

At daylight I unsaddled my mount and made a hearty breakfast of bacon and hardtack. *Then I lighted my pipe, and, making a pillow of my saddle, lay down to rest. The smoke and the fatigue of the night's journey soon made me drowsy, and before I knew it I was fast asleep. Suddenly I was awakened by a loud rumbling noise. I seized my gun instantly, and sprang toward my horse, which I had picketed in a hidden spot in the brush near by where he would be out of sight of any passing Indians. Climbing a steep hill, I looked cautiously over the country from which the noise appeared to come. There before me was a great herd of buffalo, moving at full gallop. Twenty Indians were behind it, riding hard and firing into the herd as they rode. Others near by were cutting up the carcasses of the animals that had already been killed. I saddled my horse and tied him near me. Then I crawled on my stomach to the summit of the hill, and for two hours I lay there watching the progress of the chase.*

Buffalo Bill Cody, 1920

## CHEYENNE CODY

**ABOVE:** Buffalo Bill Cody, posing with his wife, grandchildren, and friends outside of his hotel, The Irma, named after his daughter. Cody called it "just the sweetest hotel that ever was." Arguably the most famous American in the world at the turn of the century, Cody built his reputation as a hunter (killing eight buffalo a day for a year and a half), military scout, and impresario. He was instrumental in founding the town of Cody, Wyoming, where he resided until his death in 1917.

**LEFT:** Poster of Buffalo Bill's Wild West show from 1899, featuring the Rough Riders (a reference to future president Teddy Roosevelt's charge at San Juan Hill, in Cuba, during the Spanish-American War the previous year, at the head of a cavalry contingent known as the Rough Riders).

**OPPOSITE:** Invitation to the opening of Cody's hotel, The Irma, in 1902.

**OPPOSITE, INSET:** Cover of a brochure published by the Wyoming Travel Commission in the 1950s.

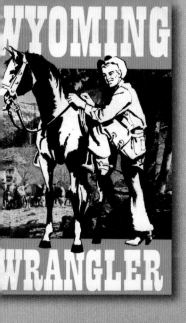

"The Irma"

Colonel W. F. Cody

earnestly desires your presence on the

Occasion of the Opening

of his new hotel

"The Irma"

at Cody, Wyoming

on the evening of November eighteenth

nineteen hundred and two

DANCING

WE WERE TO ENTER THE YELLOWSTONE FROM THE NORTH, *then the easiest route. On the way through upper Utah and across Idaho I took a few pictures. Up in Montana I made a few more pictures. . . . From Virginia City and its tired-looking Chinamen patiently reworking old gravel we moved over through Fort Ellis and established our base camp at Botelers' Ranch on the Yellowstone River. . . . There we spent three days shifting our supplies from the wagons to mule packs. Then, escorted by a small detachment of the Second United States Cavalry, we started south into the Yellowstone proper. The nearest Indians were a tribe of Crows at the agency down the river; but though they were not warlike, the government was taking no chances. . . . Late the next afternoon we had our first close view of the enchanted land, when our party came upon the Mammoth Hot Springs. We were, so far as records show, the first white men ever to see those bubbling caldrons of nature, and I found myself excited [TS—word missing here?] the knowledge that next day I was to photograph them for the first time.*

WILLIAM HENRY JACKSON, 1871

## YELLOWSTONE NATIONAL PARK

TOP LEFT: Photochrom of the lobby of the Old Faithful Inn (named after the mineral geyser and major tourist attraction in Yellowstone National Park). The giant fireplace is made of large, hand-quarried blocks of lava and weighs a total of five hundred tons.

BOTTOM LEFT: Baggage label dating from 1935, commemorating passage through the Western Entrance to Yellowstone National Park.

OPPOSITE: Mammoth Hot Springs is a large hill of travertine formed over thousands of years by hot water bubbling up and bringing calcium carbonate to the surface, where it cools and gradually accumulates into a massive deposit. This picture was taken in 1871 from one of several travertine terraces (named after such mythological deities as Jupiter and Minerva).

OVERLEAF: Shoshone Falls, on the Snake River, in Idaho, in a picture taken in 1874 by Timothy O'Sullivan, a photographer working for the U.S. Army's geological survey.

PRECEDING PAGES: Silver Gate and the Hoo-Doos, a photochrom from 1898, after an 1871 photograph by William Henry Jackson, depicting a view of Yellowstone Park. Hoodoos are tall, thin spires of rock that protrude from the bottom of arid basins and badlands.

SEE AMERICA
WELCOME TO MONTANA
UNITED STATES TRAVEL BUREAU

Far away in northwestern Montana, *hidden from view by clustering mountain-peaks, lies an unmapped corner—the Crown of the Continent. The water from the crusted snowdrift which caps the peak of a lofty mountain there trickles into tiny rills, which hurry along north, south, east, and west, and growing to rivers, at last pour their currents into three seas. From this mountain-peak the Pacific and the Arctic oceans and the Gulf of Mexico receive each its tribute. Here is a land of striking scenery. From some bold headland that rises abruptly from the plain, one looks eastward over naked yellow prairie. Near at hand, the ground is undulating, rising and falling like the swell of a troubled sea, but smooth and quiet in the far distance. . . . Here and there the yellow of the plain is broken by winding green watercourses, along which grow fringes of cottonwoods and willows, and at intervals little prairie lakes gleam like silver in the sun.*

GEORGE BIRD GRINNELL, 1901

## GLACIER NATIONAL PARK

**ABOVE:** Spectacular gelatin silver print of Glacier Park Hotel at sunrise, 1916. The panoramic photograph was copyrighted by Jacob Neitzling; this one is almost two yards long.

**OPPOSITE:** Tourists embarking on a boat in Glacier National Park. Louis Hill, president of the Great Northern Railway (and son of founder James J. Hill) decided to build Swiss-style chalets throughout the park, dubbing it "America's Switzerland."

**OPPOSITE, INSET:** "See America," a poster promoting travel to Montana, dated 1938. It was a creation of the Works Progress Administration Federal Art Project, one of Franklin Delano Roosevelt's enterprises. Many handsome "See America" posters were designed and printed during the Great Depression.

**ABOVE:** Union Pacific railway station at Gardiner, Montana, at the northern entrance to Yellowstone National Park, in 1905.

Boulder, Colorado, *lies nestling close to the Rocky Mountains just north of the 40th parallel. There the foothills are strikingly beautiful and high, and only twenty miles away Arapahoe Peak, clasping to its bosom the best glacier of the southern Rockies, gleams whitely in full view, . . . Away to the eastward the plain stretches unbrokenly, save for an occasional butte, till lost to vision. . . . [W]hat I shall remember most about Colorado is its exuberance of water. It courses down all the mountain cañons, roaring and bubbling and dashing into foam. Springs are frequent and of a pureness and coolness that make them perfect. On the plains everywhere that one goes, a ditch full to the brim runs beside one. From the top of Green Mountain a hundred lakes may be seen gleaming on the plain. It is plainly a land of abundant rain and water. And yet why this feverish haste to irrigate the fields, why these ditches, these sluices, these storage-reservoirs? Why is land with a water-right worth several hundred dollars an acre, and land without one but five dollars? And why, to ask a still deeper question, why does nearly every kind of native plant have some means of conserving water, or some contrivance for preventing too rapid transpiration? . . . It is a semi-arid land, parched and thirsty. . . . The rapid drainage, the light dry air, the fierce light of the high elevation, the hot sun, the soil unfitted for the retention of water, all these things parch and wither our cultural plants.*

Francis Potter Daniels, 1911

PRECEDING PAGES: Photochrom of Garden of the Gods, 1899, after an 1871 photograph by William Henry Jackson. Garden of the Gods is now a park on the outskirts of Colorado Springs, Colorado. The name is not, as many suppose, of Indian origin, but derived from a conversation between its two discoverers in 1859. One suggested it was a good site for a beer garden, the other answered that it was a garden fit for the gods.

OPPOSITE: In 1908 Colorado's capital city of Denver hosted the Democratic national nominating convention. The new Mizpah Arch, shown here, was built in 1906. It weighed 70 tons, was built of bronze-coated steel, and was illuminated by more than 2,000 light bulbs.

ABOVE: The Brown Palace Hotel is the second-oldest hotel in Denver. Its atrium-style structure was new and unique when it opened in 1892. There is a tradition of parading the grand champion steer from the Denver stock show through the hotel lobby during afternoon tea.

LEFT: Tourists visiting the ruins of the Boulder freight yards following a disastrous fire in 1907; fire spread to a car loaded with 2,400 pounds of dynamite.

RIGHT: Baggage sticker from the Oxford Hotel, Denver's oldest, founded in 1891.

OVERLEAF: Guests at the Brown Palace Hotel touring Red Rocks, now a park and amphitheater outside the city.

OVERLEAF, FACSIMILE: Menu for May 11, 1891, from the Antlers Hotel in Colorado Springs.

DENVER
BOULDER

U.S. SIGNAL STATION SUMMIT PIKES PEAK

# Menu.

Terrapin.
Bouillon.

Soup Sticks,             New Radishes.

Baked Bluefish—American.
Potato Croquetts,           Sliced Cucumbers.

Fried Frog Saddles.
Boiled Capon with Pork, Egg Sauce.    Cauliflower, Allemande.

Fillet of Beef, larded, Antlers,
Asparagus au beurre.

Sweetbreads braize, Mushrooms.      Spinach with Cream.

Queen Fritters, Jamaica Rum Sauce.

IMPERIAL PUNCH.

Roast Prime Ribs of Beef,      Roast Turkey Stuffed.
Mashed Potatoes.    Green Peas.    New Potatoes in Cream.

Roast Plover with Cress.

Chicken Salad.      Dressed Lettuce.

Pudding Souffle 'a la Reine, Champagne Sauce.
Peach Meringue Pie.      Pumpkin Pie.
Charlotte Russe au Maraschino.
Almond Cake,    Angel Food,    Lady Fingers,    Fancy Macaroons,
French Kisses,    Charteruse Jelly,    Port Wine Jelly.

Tutti Frutti Ice Cream.

Strawberries with Whipped Cream,
California Oranges,    Bananas,    Apples,      Mixed Nuts,
Layer Raisins,      Figs.

Roquefort,    Pine Apple and Cream Cheese,
Bent's Biscuits,      Soda Crackers,      Coffee.

COLORADO SPRINGS, COLO.
MAY 11, 1901.

THE ANTLERS,
E. BARNETT, PROPRIETOR.

STONE & LOCKE CO., DENVER.

*Colorado has its summer resort for "la high-life." It is a spa high in the Rocky Mountains, near a hot sulfur spring. As you arrive in these desolate landscapes, having traveled through grim and barren country, you are astonished at the sight of a darling little house, decorated and equipped with a degree of—dare I say it?—luxe. It even boasts a piano, whose notes echo from the mountain slopes, producing an effect that combines the mournful with the grotesque. The baths are well constructed, with large bathing pools. The savage wilderness that surrounds this spa gives it an added charm. Idle Parisians in search of novelty and out-of-the-way holidays should come here to spend their summer.*

OLYMPE AUDOUARD, 1869

## COLORADO SPRINGS
## ROYAL GORGE

**ABOVE AND OPPOSITE:** Two views of Royal Gorge, near Cañon City, Colorado. The photograph, opposite, was taken by William Henry Jackson in 1879, a year after the tracks were laid. The photochrom, above, was made from a photograph taken from the opposite side of the gorge, on the far side of the bridge; note that the stream is on the left and the rails are on the right.

The gorge is a thousand feet deep in places, and features remarkable engineering feats, such as the Hanging Bridge.

**OVERLEAF:** A Colorado Midland Railway train pushing a rotary snow plow emerges from a snow shed at Hagerman Pass in an 1899 photochrom. The Midland was an especially difficult railroad to run, with long climbs of up to 3 percent grade. In 1899 the line was closed for two-and-a-half months by a blizzard.

**ABOVE:** This 1901 photochrom depicts the summit of Pikes Peak, with the Manitou and Pikes Peak Railroad in the foreground. This cog railway has been operating since 1889.

**LEFT:** The Antlers Hotel in Colorado Springs was founded by William Jackson Palmer, who founded the town as well. The hotel's great rival was the Broadmoor, founded by millionaire Spencer Penrose, who eventually managed to gain control of the Antlers as well.

*IN THE MIDDLE AGES there was the legend of the Holy Grail. Sixty-seven years ago in Colorado there was the legend of a snowy cross upon a mountain. No man we talked with had ever seen the Mountain of the Holy Cross. But everyone knew that somewhere in the far reaches of the western highlands such a wonder might exist. Hadn't a certain hunter once caught a glimpse of it—only to have it vanish as he approached? Didn't a wrinkled Indian here and there narrow his eyes and slowly nod his head when questioned? Wasn't this man's grandfather, and that man's uncle, and old so-and-so's brother the first white man ever to lay eyes on the Holy Cross—many, many, many years ago? It was a beautiful legend, and they nursed it carefully. But anyone who wanted to see Holy Cross could climb Gray's Peak on a clear day and pick it up with field-glasses. As one comes close to the cross it always disappears behind Notch Mountain—and that is how the myth established itself.*

WILLIAM HENRY JACKSON, 1871

ASPEN
HOLY CROSS

BOTTOM LEFT: The Hotel Jerome's barbershop in the early days; note the electrical cord leading to the hairdryer by the mirror.

OPPOSITE: The 14,000-foot Mount of the Holy Cross is the northernmost mountain in Colorado's Sawatch Range, and was well known in the nineteenth century for its cross-shaped snowfield. The photographer who took this picture, William Henry Jackson, took part in the first recorded ascent of the peak, though certainly Native Americans and miners had climbed the mountain before.

ABOVE: The Hotel Jerome in Aspen, Colorado, was founded in 1899 by Jerome Wheeler, a co-owner of New York's Macy's department store. It was the finest hotel in the unruly mining town, and the first building west of the Mississippi River to be fully electrified. It fell on hard times in the "silver crash" of the 1890s.

CAME A DAY WHEN I WANTED TO GET MARRIED AND NEEDED A STAKE. *To my youthful optimism . . . the vast affluence of five dollars a day in the gold mines seemed to offer the quickest solution. I got on with the company which was leasing the workings of the old Camp Bird mine about Ouray Colorado, quite simply. My stepfather, a cattle rancher in near-by San Miguel and Montrose counties, knew the superintendent. I myself knew no miners and nothing about mining. On a bitter-cold January day I landed in Ouray. It was a gloomy little town, with down-at-the-heel brick buildings lining the main street, an astonishing rococo hotel, and rows of widely spaced, once-handsome frame houses radiating out from the remnants of the business district. Over it all hung the ineffable sadness of departed wealth. Its setting, however, is superlative; I think no town in America can boast of finer. The village lies in the bottom of an enormous rock amphitheater. The best way to see it is to stretch out flat on your back. There is only one direction in Ouray—up. The sheer watercourses, the scars cut by snowslides, the vaulting ridges—each soaring line lifts your eye irresistibly to the crenelated peaks that ring you round. Everywhere are bold smears of color. Bluish limestone low down, red and orange stratas [sic] of sandstone above them, and higher still the grays, browns, and intermediate shades of granite, porphyry and rhyolite. Threading all this are occasional streaks of bright yellow dirt. Up these brilliant flanks crawl the forests, close-crowded wherever they can find a foothold. The best places are risky enough. Scarcely a stand of timber can be seen that hasn't been mauled by avalanches. In winter the aspens tremble bare and silvery; the pines are green, and the higher spruce appear almost black against the dazzling snow. You look at all this and the village seems to shrink and shrink until it is a toy town, and you no longer notice its patheticness.*

DAVID SIEVERT LAVENDER, 1943

**OPPOSITE, TOP:** Mount Sopris, as seen from Spring Gulch Mine, south of Aspen. This photograph is undated but was probably taken around 1898. Mount Sopris is unusual in that it has two peaks, West Sopris and East Sopris, both exactly the same height: 12,965 feet.

**OPPOSITE, BOTTOM:** The *New York Times* said of this 1852 daguerreotype: "A portrait of William McKnight, a macho 49er in a red shirt with a knife tucked in his belt, is touching only when you learn from some letters he sent to his mother that he had failed as a miner and was dying of cholera at the age of 35, '500 miles away from my wife and not a person about me who would do any thing without pay.'"

**ABOVE:** Mill at the abandoned Camp Bird Mine, in Ouray County, in 1940. The Camp Bird Mine (named after the voracious birds that pecked at miners' food) was the second-richest gold mine in the state of Colorado. Owner Thomas Walsh sold it, moved east, and bought the Hope Diamond for his daughter in 1911.

**LEFT:** A burro train bringing gold from the Ouray mines in 1906.

**OVERLEAF, LEFT:** Ancient ruins in the Canyon de Chelly, photograph by Timothy O'Sullivan, 1873.

**OVERLEAF, RIGHT:** A Navajo Indian warming his hands over a fire in a tepee, photograph by William Carpenter, 1915.

BERNARD UNDERSTOOD. *He knew that once, long ago, at that hour of the day, a young Bishop had ridden along the Albuquerque road and seen Santa Fé for the first time. . . . The old town was better to look at in those days, Father Latour used to tell Bernard with a sigh. In the old days it had an individuality, a style of its own; a tawny adobe town with a few green trees, set in a half-circle of carnelian-coloured hills; that and no more. But the year 1880 had begun a period of incongruous American building. Now, half the plaza square was still adobe, and half was flimsy wooden buildings with double porches, scroll-work and jackstraw posts and banisters painted white. Father Latour said the wooden houses which had so distressed him in Ohio, had followed him. . . . Wrapped in his Indian blankets, the old Archbishop sat for a long while, looking at the open, golden face of his Cathedral. How exactly young Molny, his French architect, had done what he wanted! Nothing sensational, simply honest building and good stone-cutting,—good Midi Romanesque of the plainest. And even now, in winter, when the locust trees before the door were bare, how it was of the South, that church, how it sounded the note of the South!*

WILLA CATHER, 1927

# SANTA FE
# ALBUQUERQUE

**ABOVE:** The Hotel La Fonda in Santa Fe, 1940s. There has been an inn more or less on the site of La Fonda for some four hundred years. The hotel boasts: "award-winning pueblo style Spanish architecture and decor, with thick wooden beams, latilla ceilings, carved corbels, handcrafted chandeliers, tin and copper light fixtures and a myriad of other details created by local artisans."

**TOP RIGHT:** This 1948 advertisement for the luxury Santa Fe Super Chief, running weekly between Los Angeles and Chicago, shows an engineer waving to a boy dressed as an Indian chief. The boy, however, is not waving back.

**BOTTOM RIGHT:** Albuquerque's Fred Harvey Indian Building, adjoining the Alvarado Hotel, was built in 1902. It

contained an Indian museum. Both the hotel and the museum were demolished in 1970.

**OPPOSITE:** The Super Chief makes a stop at Albuquerque in March 1943.

**OVERLEAF:** Photographer Thomas O'Sullivan took this photograph as part of Wheeler's survey for the U.S. Army Corps of Engineers. It depicts a section of the south side of the Zuni pueblo in New Mexico, 1873.

IT IS HARD TO REALIZE THAT THE FIRST AMERICAN SETTLEMENT WAS MADE IN THIS PLACE IN 1868, *and that all this transformation has taken place in the short interval of about twenty years. Then the sun beat down upon an arid plain covered with greasewood, mesquite, and cactus, and its rays served only to scorch the struggling vegetation. A narrow strip of verdure marked the presence of the river and relieved the eye from the glare of the desert. It would be hard to find a more perfect picture of nature in her wildest and most savage mood. Now great fields of wheat and barley stretch away for miles, acres upon acres of alfalfa gladden the eye, and orchards are found on every hand.... In addition, the sugar cane and the cotton plant thrive in these rich valleys, and it would be unfair to omit any reference to the native plants, many of which would provide a profitable source of revenue if cultivated.... Among these are the maguey, or mescal.... From it a distilled liquor is made containing a large percentage of alcohol. It is as clear as gin, and has the strong, smoky taste of Scotch whisky, and will intoxicate as quickly as either.*

THE NEW YORK TIMES, 1890

PHOENIX

TOP: The Biltmore is one of the most prestigious hotels in Phoenix, Arizona, and its neighborhood is known as the Biltmore district. It was designed by the hotel's first owner, Albert McArthur, but the fact that Frank Lloyd Wright consulted on the project for four months in 1928 has given rise to numerous attributions of the building to Wright. The hotel opened in 1929, not the best of times economically, and sure enough the McArthur brothers lost the hotel to their investors the following year. The hotel is still a Phoenix attraction, and is now a Hilton property.

LEFT: Lobby of the Biltmore when it was brand new, in the early 1930s.

In the great desert of northern Arizona the traveller, *threading his way across a sage-brush and cacti plain shut in by abrupt-sided shelves of land rising here and there some hundreds of feet higher, suddenly comes upon a petrified forest. Trunks of trees in all stages of fracture strew the ground over a space some miles in extent. So perfect are their forms, he is almost minded to think the usual wasteful wood-chopper has been by and left the scattered products of his art in littered confusion upon the scene of his exploit. Only their beautiful color conveys a sense of strangeness to the eye, and leaning down and touching them, he finds that they are—stone. Chalcedony, not carbon! Form has outlived substance and kept the resemblance, while the particles of the original matter have all been spirited away. Yet so perfect is the presentment, one can hardly believe the fact, and where one fallen giant spans a barren cañon, one almost thinks to hear the sound of water rushing down the creek. But it is some millions of years and more since this catastrophe befell, and the torrent, uprooting it, left it prone, with limbs outstretched in futile grasp upon the other side. A conifer it was, cousin only to such as grow to-day, and flourished probably in the Cretaceous era; for the land has not been under water here since the advent of Tertiary times.*

PERCIVAL LOWELL, 1908

## PETRIFIED FOREST

OPPOSITE: Edward Curtis was a renowned documenter of Indian history, life, and ways. In 1906 J. P. Morgan agreed to fund an ambitious new project to photograph and document the Indians, and this photograph of three Arizona Qahatika women walking through the desert after a hasen harvest, one with a pot on her head and two with kiho carriers on theirs, was taken the following year, 1907. That same year, Curtis wrote: "The information that is to be gathered . . . respecting the mode of life of one of the great races of mankind, must be collected at once or the opportunity will be lost."

ABOVE This 1898 photochrom shows the Agate Bridge, in Arizona's Petrified Forest, near Adamana. Floodwaters washed out an arroyo, or gully, underneath this 110-foot petrified log, which resisted erosion while the softer rock beneath it washed away.
LEFT: This 1898 photochrom depicts a Navajo Indian weaving a blanket.

THE CANYON HAD CHANGED AGAIN *from one which was very narrow to one much more complex, greater, and grander. The walls on top were many miles apart; Comanche Point, to our left, was over 4000 feet above us; Desert View, Moran Point, and other points on the south rim were even higher. On the right we could see an arch near Cape Final on Greenland Point, over 5000 feet up, that we had photographed, from the top, a few years before. Pagoda-shaped temples—the formation so typical of the Grand Canyon—clustered on all sides. The upper walls were similar in tint to those in Marble Canyon, but here at the river was a new formation; the algonkian, composed of thousands of brilliantly coloured bands of rock, standing at an angle—the one irregularity to the uniform layers of rock—a remnant of thousands of feet of rock which once covered this region, then was planed away before the other deposits were placed. All about us, close to the river, was a deep, soft sand formed by the disintegration of the rocks above, as brilliantly coloured as the rocks from which they came. What had been a very narrow stream above here spread out over a thousand feet wide, ran with a good current, and seemed to be anything but a shallow stream at that.*

ELLSWORTH LEONARDSON KOLB AND EMORY CLIFFORD KOLB, 1914

## GRAND CANYON

PRECEDING PAGES: On the "Zig Zags," an especially steep section of the Grand Canyon's Bright Angel trail renowned for its switchbacks, a 1900 photochrom based on an 1875 photograph by William Henry Jackson.

OPPOSITE: Ellsworth and Emery Kolb were a pair of enterprising brothers who built a career on photography and the Grand Canyon. In 1911 they descended the Colorado River through the Grand Canyon and made a motion picture of it, an unprecedented achievement. This photograph of a man and a donkey out on Tanner Ledge dates from 1913. Note the man's odd helmet.

ABOVE LEFT: Baggage label from the Pioneer Hotel, the eleven-story pride of Tucson, built at the end of the 1920s.

ABOVE RIGHT: The El Tovar Hotel, built just twenty feet from the edge of the Grand Canyon's south rim, opened its doors in 1905.

RIGHT: Posed photograph illustrating the "dangers" of the Grand Canyon's precipice.

OVERLEAF: The Moki Snake Dance, shown here in a 1902 photochrom, is an old and remarkable ceremony practiced among the Pueblo Indians of Arizona.

THE VIVID PINK CLIFF, *which, had it not long since been washed away from Little Zion, would have added another tier of color to its top, here, on the desert, remains a distant horizon. The road climbs Lake Bonneville's southern shore, and, at Cedar City, reaches the glorified sandstones. From Cedar City to the canyon one sweeps through Mormon settlements founded more than sixty years ago, a region of stream-watered valleys known of old as Dixie. The road is part of the Arrowhead Trail, once in fact a historic trail, now a motor-highway between Salt Lake and Los Angeles. The valleys bloom. Pomegranates, figs, peaches, apricots, melons, walnuts, and almonds reach a rare perfection. Cotton, which Brigham Young started here as an experiment in 1861, is still grown. Lusty cottonwood-trees line the banks of the little rivers. Cedars dot the valleys and cover thickly the lower hills. And everywhere, on every side, the arid cliffs close in. The Pink Cliff has been left behind, but the Vermilion Cliff constantly appears. The White Cliff enters and stays. Long stretches of road overlie one and another colored stratum; presently the ground is prevailingly red, with here and there reaches of mauve, yellow, green, and pink.*

ROBERT STERLING YARD, 1919

ZION NATIONAL PARK
BRYCE CANYON

ABOVE: Poster for the Ranger Naturalist Service in Zion National Park, dated 1938, a Works Progress Administration creation, offering "field trips, campfire programs, natural history talks & exhibits, general information." Zion Canyon was probably named by the explorer John Wesley Powell, who visited here in the early 1870s. One earlier explorer of the canyon, Joseph Black, was mocked for his description of Zion's beauty; locals referred to the canyon as "Joseph's Glory."

ABOVE: Logo from a paper bag from Bryce Canyon National Park, Utah.
OPPOSITE: Pulpit Rock, in Utah's Echo Canyon, in a turn-of-the-century photochrom based on an earlier photograph by William Henry Jackson. Note the railroad tracks running just below the pulpit-shaped boulder.

PERHAPS NINETEEN TWENTIETHS OF THE HOUSES ARE BUILT OF BLUISH-GRAY ADOBE BRICKS, *and are only one or two stories high, forming fine cottage homes which promise simple comfort within. They are set well back from the street, leaving room for a flower garden, while almost every one has a thrifty orchard at the sides and around the back. The gardens are laid out with great simplicity, indicating love for flowers by people comparatively poor, rather than deliberate efforts of the rich for showy artistic effects. They are like the pet gardens of children, about as artless and humble, and harmonize with the low dwellings to which they belong. In almost every one you find daisies, and mint, and lilac bushes, and rows of plain English tulips. Lilacs and tulips are the most characteristic flowers, and nowhere have I seen them in greater perfection. As Oakland is preeminently a city of roses, so is this Mormon Saints' Rest a city of lilacs and tulips. The flowers, at least, are saintly, and they are surely loved. Scarce a home, however obscure, is without them, and the simple, unostentatious manner in which they are planted and gathered in pots and boxes about the windows shows how truly they are prized.*

JOHN MUIR, 1877

TEMPLE SQUARE
in Salt Lake City

*Compliments*
TEMPLE SQUARE
BUREAU OF INFORMATION

**OPPOSITE:** Eagle Gate, in Salt Lake City, photographed in 1900, was the original entrance to the estate of Mormon prophet Brigham Young. Despite the presence of the eagle, the official state bird is the seagull: seagulls are drawn this far inland by the enormous salt lake, and seagulls devoured a plague of locusts that threatened to destroy the 1848 crop of the early Mormon settlers.

**ABOVE:** In this photochrom of about 1900, the Old Tithing House is the *Deseret Evening News* Building.
**LEFT:** Brochure of Temple Square from the 1950s. The Salt Lake Temple, one of the chief shrines of the Mormon religion, was completed in the early 1890s, exactly forty years after Mormon prophet Brigham Young laid the cornerstone.
**OVERLEAF:** The SaltAir Pavilion was built in 1893 just outside of Salt Lake City. It was intended as the western counterpart to Coney Island, and was morally impeccable and family friendly, in keeping with Mormon strictures.

SALT LAKE CITY

You soon discover that Reno is Reno, wonderfully and singularly itself. . . . *It is a throw-back to the hard, tough, roomy epoch of the gold rush and the mining camp. Its free-and-easy manners belong to its tradition. Gambling is in its blood. Reno derives from the lustiest and most boisterous episode in the American Iliad; it is the true descendant of Virginia City, Silver City, Goldfield, of rifled glory holes and big bonanzas. . . . If Reno is typical of anything—and this is what makes interesting its easy divorcing, its open gambling, its simple cynicism—it is of something native to this land which the most regulatory laws in the world have never succeeded in regulating. Reno is the frontier and what the frontier has always stood for: Puritans running away from Puritans.*

ANNE O'HARE MCCORMICK, 1931

RENO

LEFT: Eddie's Fabulous 50's Casino and Diner; detail of a photograph from the late 1980s.

OPPOSITE: The Virginia Street location of Harrah's Bingo, from 1938 to 1945, was the third Harrah's in Reno's history. The club doubled its size when it moved to this location, adjoining Harold's Club. A door connected the two establishments so that drinks from Harold's could be served in the bingo parlor.

FACSIMILE: Harold Smith, owner of Harold's Club, dealing cards, 1940s.

OVERLEAF: Map of Sacramento; this bird's-eye view was published by the *Daily Record-Union* and *Weekly Union*, Sacramento papers in the second half of the nineteenth century. The map features important public buildings, such as the Bank Corp., the County Hospital, the Hall of Records, the State Capitol, the Court House, and the Western Hotel.

ABOVE: The Reno Arch was built in 1927, but it took several more years before the slogan "The Biggest Little City in the World" emerged from a public contest, with a $100 grand prize. The neon lettering and twin torches were installed on the arch in 1929, but as a result of complaints from Renoites, it was removed in 1934. The arch marked the completion of two major highway routes.

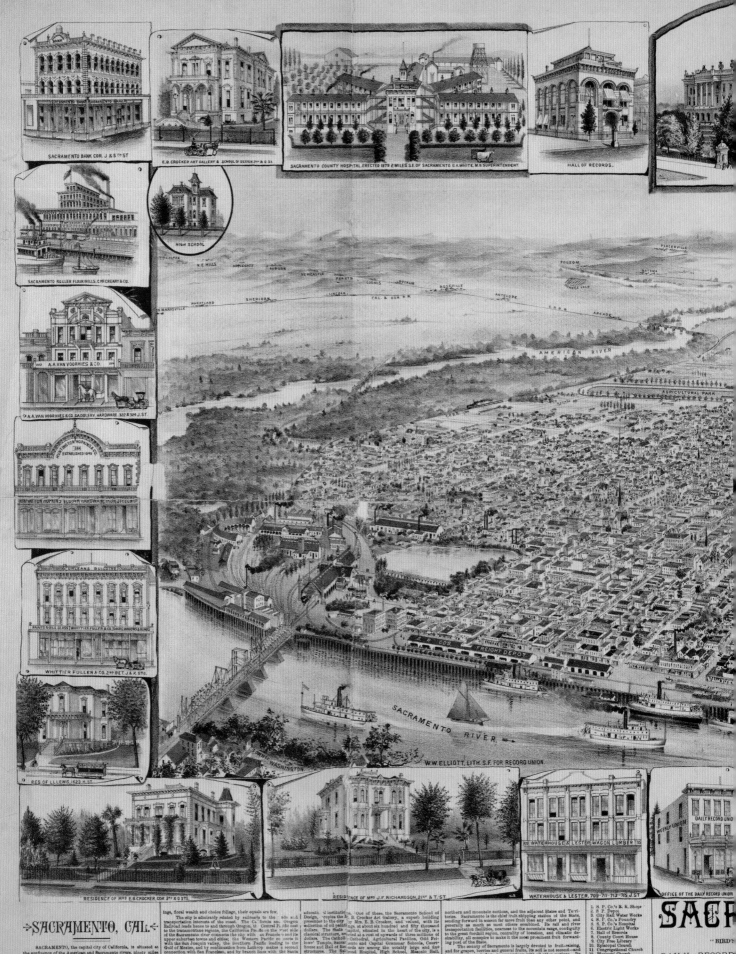

GROUPE OF STATUARY PRESENTED BY O.D. MILLS ESQ.

DRY GOODS DEPARTMENT.

INTERIOR VIEWS OF WEINSTOCK & LUBIN GENERAL OUTFITTERS.

WESTERN HOTEL Wm LAND. PROP. 209 TO 211 K ST.

COURT HOUSE.

GRAMMAR SCHOOL

PIONEER MILLING COMPANY.

BOOTH & CO. WHOLESALE GROCERS.

RES OF L. TOZER COR 15TH & H ST

BASSETT & MUNFORD PROP FRONT & O LTS

RES. OF C.H. CUMMINGS COR G & NINTH STS.

COPYRIGHTED.

INTERIOR VIEW OF REAL ESTATE OFFICE OF EDWIN K. ALSIP & CO. SACRAMENTO CAL.

EDWIN K. ALSIP & CO. REAL ESTATE

ORANGE VALE 15 MILES FROM SACRAMENTO.

RESIDENCE OF JOSEPH STEFFENS COR H & 16TH ST.

MENTO.

PUBLISHED BY THE

AND WEEKLY UNION

Journals of the Pacific Coast.

Weekly $2.00 per year."

22. Crocker Art Gallery
23. Capital Grammar School
24. High School
25. First Baptist Church
26. Clunie Opera House
27. Odd Fellows Temple
28. Turner Hall
29. Catholic Cathedral
30. German Lutheran Church
31. City Plaza
32. State Capitol
33. State Exposition Building
34. State Printing Office
35. Grammar School
36. Sutter's Old Fort
37. "Nob Hill"
38. Town of Enterprise
39. City Cemetery
A. "Nama Colony"
A. Street Railways
B. Electric Railway

ORANGE VALE.—The lands of the Orange Vale Colonization Company, are situated north of the American River, sixteen miles from Sacramento, two miles from Folsom, and eight miles from Roseville, the junction of the C.P. & C. & O. railroads.

OAK PARK, as represented in the above view, is located on the southeastern boundary of the city, and embraces a tract of 380 acres, of which, a portion has been subdivided into villa lots 50x150 feet, with broad avenues, graded and lined with palms, magnolia and other semi-tropical trees.

[T]HEN UP THE SIERRA NEVADA, PINES, STARS, MOUNTAIN LODGES SIGNIFYING FRISCO ROMANCES . . . *I suddenly realized I was in California. Warm, palmy air—air you can kiss—and palms. Along the storied Sacramento River on a superhighway; into the hills again; up, down; and suddenly the vast expanse of bay (it was just before dawn) with the sleepy lights of Frisco festooned across. Over the Oakland Bay Bridge I slept soundly for the first time since Denver; so that I was rudely jolted in the bus station at Market and Fourth into the memory of the fact that I was three thousand two hundred miles from my aunt's house in Paterson, New Jersey. I wandered out like a haggard ghost, and there she was, Frisco—long, bleak streets with trolley wires all shrouded in fog and whiteness.*

JACK KEROUAC, 1950S

## SAN FRANCISCO

ABOVE: An 1884 photograph of the 450-square-mile San Francisco Bay at sunset, by photographer George Fiske, who moved west in 1879. He took many photographs of California wildlife, and photographer Ansel Adams owned a book of Fiske's photographs when he was a boy. That book led him to visit Yosemite National Park, where Adams did much of his finest work.

LEFT: View of silver-mining millionaire Adolph Sutro's seven-story Victorian château, Cliff House, 1902. This magnificent building, also known as the Gingerbread Palace, was erected in the wake of the fire that destroyed the first Cliff House in 1894. It in turn burned to the ground in 1907, despite having survived the 1906 earthquake and fire.

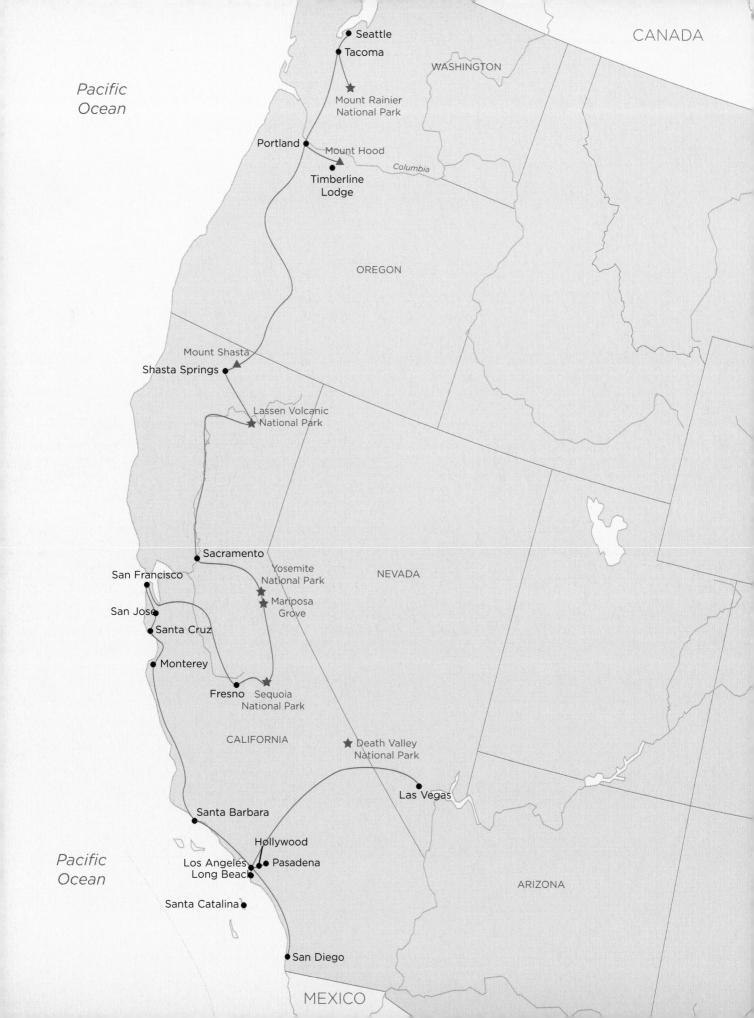

Pacific
Ocean

CANADA

WASHINGTON

Seattle
Tacoma

Mount Rainier
National Park

Portland • Mount Hood
Timberline
Lodge

Columbia

OREGON

Mount Shasta
Shasta Springs

Lassen Volcanic
National Park

Sacramento

San Francisco

Yosemite
National Park

NEVADA

San Jose

Santa Cruz

Mariposa
Grove

Monterey

Fresno

Sequoia
National Park

CALIFORNIA

Death Valley
National Park

Las Vegas

Santa Barbara

Hollywood

Pacific
Ocean

Los Angeles
Long Beach

Pasadena

ARIZONA

Santa Catalina

San Diego

MEXICO

Visitors to Seattle in the early part of the twentieth century knew they were in a boomtown; timber barons, gold tycoons, and shipping magnates built magnificent homes and public institutions of all sorts here. Seattle was San Francisco's chief rival on the Pacific coast, and even after the Panic of 1893 undercut the city's spectacular growth, the Alaskan gold rush kept the city jumping.

Seattle was the chief port for the Alaska trade. As a port, it also took in rice, silk, tea, spices, indigo, and other products from Asia. Last but not least, it exported salmon, the magnificent emblem of the Pacific Northwest. Travelers to this part of the world after the construction of the Grand Coulee and the Bonneville dams (work on Bonneville extended from 1909 to 1934, the Grand Coulee was built during the 1930s) would often travel out to see the salmon ladders. In his book *Inside USA*, John Gunther described the salmon ladders as "among the most ingenious things I have ever seen, and to watch the salmon climb them is a unique experience." During the spawning season as many as 30,000 salmon thrash their way to the top of the dam each day.

Gunther also described the water flowing over the dam itself: "The water breaks over in a smooth green moving wall, and then bursts into a churning foam of white. The green water sliding down is solid and smooth like a broad conveyor belt. Eleven blindingly white waterfalls intersect the swelling bulge and, propelled forward as if by giant hoses, spill out and down. The white curtain of spray is 30 feet thick, and the roar of the mixing waters can be heard for miles."

Visitors to Seattle necessarily reached it by ship or by rail. If by rail from points east, they probably took James J. Hill's Great Northern line through the Cascade Mountains and would have been constantly reminded that rail travel was anything but routine and entirely safe. In 1910 a Great Northern passenger train waiting out a blizzard on a siding was swept away by an avalanche; it was the worst rail disaster in American history. The Cascades are dramatic, beautiful, and treacherous.

The train running south from Seattle passes through Portland, Oregon, in the shadow of Mount Hood. Notoriously, Manhattan was sold by the Indians for 24 dollars, but half the 640-acre claim to the site of Portland was sold in 1835 for 25 cents. The name of the city was decided by a coin toss. These

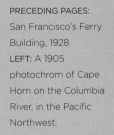

RIGHT: This 1939 Chicago and North Western Line timetable features three generations of locomotives from steam to the modern streamlined diesel.
BELOW: Crown Point and Vista House, on the Northwest Pacific's Columbia River Gorge, about 1916. The spectacular view from the Vista House was one of America's earliest great tourist attractions.

details of Pacific Northwest history give some sense of the rough-and-ready nature of the last mainland frontier.

Side trips in the Pacific Northwest include the Columbia River Gorge, where one of the early landmarks and purpose-built tourist attractions was Crown Point Vista House. It was built in conjunction with the Columbia River Highway. According to the engineer who designed that highway, the rocky Crown Point promontory, 733 feet above the Columbia River, was the ideal site for "an observatory from which the view both up and down the Columbia could be viewed in silent communion with the infinite." Construction on the Vista House began in 1918.

Another side trip is to Crater Lake, which lies inside the caldera, or basin, of a dormant volcano. Filled by rainwater, the six-by-five-mile lake is an unearthly cerulean blue. Another otherworldly feature is a piece of driftwood known as the "Old Man of the Lake"—a tall tree stump, thirty feet long by two feet wide, that has been bobbing vertically in the lake at least since 1896. Farther south is California's Lassen Volcanic National Park. Visitors in 1915 were treated to Mt. Lassen's last recorded eruption.

Although the rail lines nowadays are largely inland, there were some sections that ran along the dramatic northern California coast. But it was motorists who most enjoyed the spectacular, mist-wreathed coastal bluffs. Trains pulling into San Francisco from the north deposited their passengers at ferry terminals along the shores of the San Francisco Bay. They would then take ferries to the fog-shrouded city by the bay.

San Francisco has long been famous for many different features: the steep hills (one anonymous wit said, "When you get tired of walking around in San Francisco, you can always lean against it"), the beautiful vistas (Susan Cheever wrote, "When you drive up over 19th Avenue and see the bridge rising before you, it's like seeing the towers of Chartres when you're driving out of Paris"), and the writhing fog. Perhaps Frank Lloyd Wright said it most adroitly: "What I like best about San Francisco is San Francisco."

ABOVE: This 1905 photochrom of the California Ltd. in the Mojave Desert features cactus and Joshua trees. The California Ltd., the "Finest Train West of Chicago," ran regular service from that city to Los Angeles from 1892 to 1954. RIGHT: Baggage label from The Californian (1936).

Rita Hayworth imprinted a memorable image when she coyly remarked: "I like the way the wind whips your skirts when you go by cable-car up Nob Hill," while Erroll Flynn reinforced his own mystique by saying: "I always see about six scuffles a night when I come to San Francisco," finishing with a flourish: "That's one of the town's charms."

Guy Murchie, aviator and philosopher, described flying over the fog-cloaked city by night: "Once I saw San Francisco blinking up at me through such a mottled shroud that it seemed the hidden heart of a strange planet. Car and street lights of every color flashed on and off in weird contrapuntal rhythm through holes and thin spots of the moving fog. If one had descended upon Saturn or Pluto to behold a similar sight I can imagine the awe it would inspire."

From San Francisco, one can head east to Yosemite, Kings Canyon, and Sequoia national parks. Perhaps Ansel Adams, the legendary nature photographer, described Yosemite best: "Yosemite Valley, to me, is always a sunrise, a glitter of green and golden wonder in a vast edifice of stone and space."

Head south from San Francisco, and you travel through the sun-kissed hills and along the windswept coasts of California. There is no place quite like it on the planet—and certainly no place has ever been so insistently and professionally photographed.

Californians—according to a history of the state entitled *Inventing the Dream*—thought of the southern portion of their state as the Mediterranean of North America, a compendium of Greece, Italy, and southern France that would become the cultural center of the nation, and one day, the world. And in a sense, perhaps, it did.

It is possible to write about the glamour, the wealth, and the sheer physical beauty of L.A., but Raymond Chandler, it has been said, "wrote like a slumming angel and invested the sun-blinded streets of Los Angeles with a romantic presence."

Another observer of Southern California, Carey McWilliams, wrote: "God never intended Southern California to be anything but desert . . . Man has made it what it is." Certainly, had it not been for the deviation of the Colorado River and the devastation of the Owens Valley (events referenced in the movie *Chinatown*), Los Angeles could never have existed. But those great works of engineering were completed, and Los Angeles flourishes in what was once an arid waste.

Carey McWilliams and so many others who take gratuitous shots at the odd and beautiful place that is the second-largest city in the United States continue to congregate there.

McWilliams described the day he fell in love with Los Angeles. He was sitting in Pershing Square early one morning, dressed (uncharacteristically) in a tuxedo, struggling with a hangover, and watching the local denizens bestir themselves: "There neither was nor would ever be another place like this City of the Angels. Here the American people were erupting, like lava from a volcano; here, indeed, was the place for me—a ringside seat at the circus."

If Los Angeles has a circus-sideshow air, the product of a bouncy, exuberant entertainment industry and a long tradition of visionary spiritual movements, San Diego, further down the coast, has always preserved a blend of leisured elegance and a dreamy, ethereal quality. Edwin Markham, in a book entitled *California the Wonderful*, wrote the following about San Diego in 1914, "The glamor of antiquity hovers about San Diego, a glamor that is lit up by the bright spirit of to-day. Here the first explorers, beating up the coast of Lower California, the coast of tears and pearls, turned in at the Silver Gate and rested in the Harbor of the Sun. Here also in the early years came Junipero Serra, gentle priest and empire builder, with his sailors and soldiers, to lay foundations for an adventure of love. Here still stands a broken facade of the old cathedral, and here the first palms planted by the friars still lift their leafy heads to the sun." Markham evokes a dusty, Spanish-speaking world, the earliest days of both San Diego and the southern Pacific coast. Here is his description of San Diego's pioneer times: "Scattered over the beaches and mesas of San Diego were the low adobe homes of settlers, homes with red-tiled roofs and with walls washed with buff or blue or pale rose. Here rode the *caballeros* with jingling spur, or touched the tinkling guitar under the latticed windows where sat the dark-eyed senoritas with embroidery in hand and rose in hair." And as the city grew, climbing up the hills: "The wharves, the factories and the business houses border the water-front; while mounting back to the hills rise a flock of handsome modern homes, which have an outlook to far horizons, sweeping in the harbor and the silver belt of Coronado, with a fringe of the shores of California and a faint glimpse of the misty mountains of Mexico."

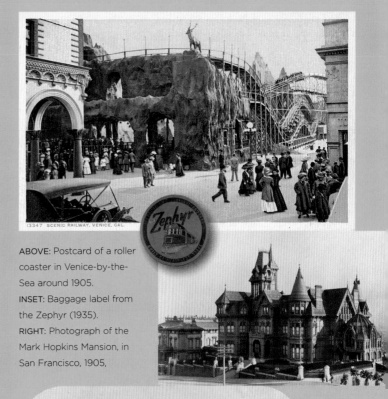

ABOVE: Postcard of a roller coaster in Venice-by-the-Sea around 1905.
INSET: Baggage label from the Zephyr (1935).
RIGHT: Photograph of the Mark Hopkins Mansion, in San Francisco, 1905,

ABOVE: This 1912 stereoscopic view (or half of one) shows grapes being set out to dry and become raisins, in California's Central Valley, 1912.
RIGHT: 1905 postcard of the Cawston Ostrich farm, in South Pasadena, California. One visitor in 1904 wrote: "The big fellows make a practice of grabbing at anything that glistens in the sun, and would as soon swallow a diamond stud or gold badge as a bite of apple or orange."

THERE ARE SO MANY FINE TRIPS TO BE TAKEN AROUND SEATTLE; *both by land and by water. Puget Sound, "the inland sea," with its islands, its inlets, and its canals and bays. I don't wonder the Scandinavians flock to this country by the thousands for it must make them think of their own country. Puget Sound's bays and inlets are like their fjords only much more pronounceable. . . . You writers and poets of the East, well written out, who cannot find new plots nor romances, go to the unsequestered spots, the out-of-the-way places along Puget Sound and you will find enough to keep you busy for a while. There are stories there well worth writing. The dark firs and hemlock, spruce and cedars hide many a tale of woe with a real live hero or heroine. I heard a Seattle man once say laughingly: "We never think of asking what a person's real name is out here," or sometimes we will say jokingly: "By the way what was your name in the East?"*

ANNETTE FITCH-BREWER, 1913

SEATTLE

RIGHT: Seattle's Second Avenue in 1907. This thoroughfare is crowded with trolley cars, and lined with advertisements and billboards; note the Owl Cigars ad.
OPPOSITE: The Hotel Sorrento was one of the more elegant hotels in pre–World War II Seattle, but Interstate 5 cut it off from downtown after the war. The construction of Freeway Park over the highway brought the Sorrento back into contact with the rest of the city; now over a century old, the Sorrento is still the grand dame of Seattle's luxury hotels.

ABOVE: Unloading reindeer in Seattle, 1898. This is the right-hand photograph of a pair of 1898 stereoscopic images by Benjamin Lloyd Singley. When it was feared that starvation was looming in the Klondike as a result of the 1897 gold rush, the U.S. government decided to pay to import 500 reindeer from Norway. They were shipped across the Atlantic, sent to the Pacific coast by rail, and transported from there to Alaska, by which time they were no longer needed.

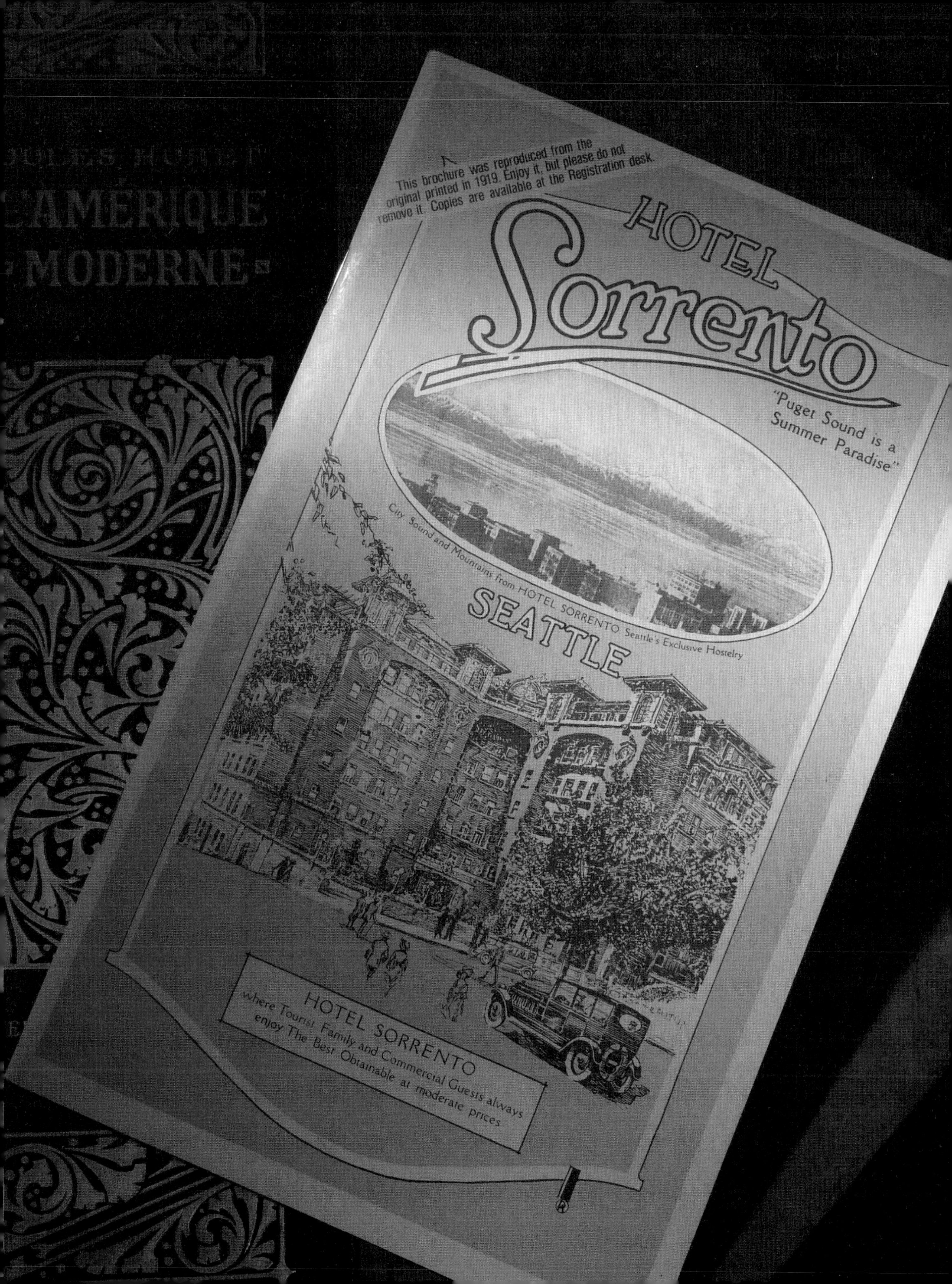

AMÉRIQUE
MODERNE
This brochure was reproduced from the original printed in 1919. Enjoy it, but please do not remove it. Copies are available at the Registration desk.
HOTEL
Sorrento
"Puget Sound is a Summer Paradise"
City Sound and Mountains from HOTEL SORRENTO Seattle's Exclusive Hostelry
SEATTLE
HOTEL SORRENTO
where Tourist Family and Commercial Guests always enjoy The Best Obtainable at moderate prices

[T]HE GRANDEST EXCURSION OF ALL TO BE MADE HEREABOUTS IS TO MOUNT RAINIER, *to climb to the top of its icy crown. . . .*
*Last summer I gained the summit from the south side, in a day and a half from the timber-line, without encountering any*
*desperate obstacles. . . . From the top of the moraine, still ascending, we passed for a mile or two through a forest of mixed*
*growth, mainly silver fir, Patton spruce, and mountain pine, and then came to the charming park region, at an elevation of*
*about five thousand feet above sea-level. . . . Every one of these parks, great and small, is a garden filled knee-deep with*
*fresh, lovely flowers of every hue, the most luxuriant and the most extravagantly beautiful of all the alpine gardens I ever*
*beheld in all my mountain-top wanderings. . . . We arrived at the Cloud Camp at noon, but no clouds were in sight, save a*
*few gauzy ornamental wreaths adrift in the sunshine. Out of the forest at last there stood the mountain, wholly unveiled,*
*awful in bulk and majesty, filling all the view like a separate, newborn world.*

JOHN MUIR, 1918

## MOUNT RAINIER

ABOVE LEFT: One of a stereoscopic pair of 1906 photographs showing a group of hikers near a waterfall in the Cascade Range, on the trail to Paradise Valley, an especially scenic section of Mount Rainier National Park.
ABOVE RIGHT: Again, a picture from a stereoscopic pair of 1906 photographs depicting Pinnacle Peak, the second-highest peak in the Tatoosh Range, rising 6,562 feet above sea level. Most of the party shown is comprised of women.

LEFT: Indian Henry is a section of Mount Rainier National Park; this photograph of a camping party there dates from the 1910s.
OPPOSITE: Group of men and women climbing Paradise Glacier on the southeastern flank of Mount Rainier, in Washington State, 1910s. Note the prevalence of women in the party.

AT THE UPPER CASCADES THE STEAMER DISCHARGES HER PASSENGERS, *on the Washington side of the river, and here a short portage of six miles by railroad is made before reembarking on another steamer to pursue the journey to Portland. . . . Approaching Portland by river, the traveler soon becomes aware that he is nearing a commercial city. River craft of all sorts and sizes, as well as ocean vessels, are found at the wharves of the city itself, one hundred and twenty-five miles from the ocean, representing the commerce of the world. East Indiamen, that have abandoned their former trade to steamers and the Suez Canal; ocean steamers, from the magnificent 3,000-ton passenger and freight steamships of the Oregon Railway and Navigation Company, to the business-looking colliers from Puget Sound, and the steam schooner that trades along the coast. These, and all sorts of river and coasting craft, are at Portland wharves. At the sight of them the fact is at once recognized that the journey across the continent is ended, and that the metropolis of the Pacific Northwest has been reached.*

HENRY JACOB WINSER, 1883

## PORTLAND

**TOP:** Panoramic view of the Willamette River in Portland, Oregon, in 1908.

**LEFT:** Passengers throng the decks of two steamboats, the *Bailey Gatzert* (right) and the *Charles R. Spencer* (foreground), in the Cascade Locks, in 1906. The 90-foot-wide, 463-foot-long Cascade Canal and Locks were completed in 1896. By then, railroad lines dominated freight traffic throughout the Pacific Northwest. In 1938 the Cascade Canal and Locks were inundated by rising water behind Bonneville Dam. The *Charles R. Spencer,* built in 1901, was owned by independent steamboat operator Captain E. W. Spencer. Both of the boats were known as fast watercraft, and they often raced through the canals.

**ABOVE LEFT:** Luggage label from the North Western–Union Pacific Railroad, 1935.

**OPPOSITE:** A photochrom of a steamboat on the Columbia River, near the Cascades, 1901.

**OPPOSITE, INSET:** Postcard packet of the Columbia River Highway, 1950s.

COLUMBIA
RIVER
*Highway*
Crown Point and Vista House

## TIMBERLINE LODGE

**PRECEDING PAGES:** A photochrom of Oregon's Mt. Hood as seen from Lost Lake, 1900. Now a national forest, Lost Lake is more than 3,000 feet up the slopes of Mount Hood.

**TOP:** View of the Timberline Lodge on Mount Hood, Oregon. The lodge was built in the late 1930s at an elevation of 6,000 feet by the federal government as part of the Works Progress Administration. A popular ski resort and wilderness hotel, it is especially well known from the opening sequences of Stanley Kubrick's *The Shining*, where it appeared under the name Overlook Hotel.

**LEFT:** Oregon postcard packet, mid-1950s.

**RIGHT:** Brochure for the Timberline Lodge, from 1941.

**OPPOSITE:** Guestroom in the Timberline Lodge, 1940s.

THIS TIMBERLINE LODGE MARKS A VENTURE THAT WAS MADE POSSIBLE BY W.P.A., EMERGENCY RELIEF WORK, *in order that we may test the workability of recreational facilities installed by the Government itself and operated under its complete control. Here, to Mount Hood, will come thousands and thousands of visitors in the coming years. Looking east toward eastern Oregon with its great livestock raising areas, these visitors are going to visualize the relationship between the cattle ranches and the summer ranges in the forests. Looking westward and northward toward Portland and the Columbia River, with their great lumber and other wood using industries, they will understand the part which National Forest timber will play in the support of this important element of northwestern prosperity. Those who will follow us to Timberline Lodge on their holidays and vacations will represent the enjoyment of new opportunities for play in every season of the year. I mention specially every season of the year because we, as a nation, I think, are coming to realize that the summer is not the only time for play. I look forward to the day when many, many people from this region of the Nation are going to come here for skiing and tobogganing and various other forms of winter sports.*

FRANKLIN DELANO ROOSEVELT, 1937

Shasta Springs hotel and the cottages clustering about it *stand high above and almost overhang the railway station. We found the pine-scented air deliciously cool and the surroundings restful. As soon as we had checked our suit cases, left an order for luncheon later, and despatched some post cards, we went out to see what we could see. An alluring path led us down the mountain side. Down and down through shady woods, zigzagging back and forth across a hurrying, foaming stream, we followed it. But the hurrying stream bade us to loiter along its way, listen to its music, and feast our eyes upon the lovely mosses, lichens and ferns that decked its banks. . . . Eagerly our eyes tried to follow the thousand rivulets hurrying, scurrying, uniting, dividing, racing as if alive through yielding green obstructions, seeking outlets by which they might escape the snares man had laid to catch and imprison them in commercial bottles. We strayed into a curiosity shop to buy some photographs, but the mental pictures that I had been "taking" all the morning I preferred to any work of a camera.*

MIRIAM McGUIRE, 1915

## SHASTA SPRINGS

**TOP:** This panoramic photograph is captioned: "Train De Luxe from New York, en route N.E.L.A. [National Electric Light Association] convention at Seattle, 1912, Shasta Springs, Calif." The National Electric Light Association was an industry group representing the interests of the growing electrification of the United States—an organization of very prosperous and powerful individuals. This trainload of attendees was on its way north to Seattle when they stopped at Shasta Springs, a very popular summer resort of the period. Waterfalls are visible from the main line of the Southern Pacific Railroad tracks that run through the town, so this photograph was probably taken to

the distant sound of roaring water.
**LEFT:** Photograph of a Southern Pacific Railroad train stopped at Shasta Springs station, 1905.
**OPPOSITE:** One of a pair of stereoscopic photographs showing the "construction of snow cover," or snow sheds, over the tracks of the Central Pacific Railroad in California's Sierra Nevada Mountains, c. 1865. This was part of the construction of the transcontinental railroad (1865–69), in the immediate aftermath of the Civil War. Snow sheds were crucial to the operation of trains through the snowy Sierra Nevadas. Note the ghostly figure of a Chinese laborer in the foreground. Perhaps he was told to get back to work before the exposure could be completed.

ON A STILL DAY MAY BE HEARD THE ROAR OF INNUMERABLE WATERFALLS *that beat themselves into a white spray against the rough, charred banks of the river courses. When no obscuring haze intervenes, or the clouds do not envelop the crags of Mt. Lassen's kingly domain, a scene of surpassing grandeur blends into the horizon in every direction. Prospect Peak near the northern rim of the old crater contains an almost perfect cone in itself. This peak in unison of action with twenty-seven other volcanoes is held responsible for the wonderful Modoc Lava Beds which spread over miles of territory. The flow cooled in undulating waves which have oxidized at the crest and now show all of the rich coloring of a Persian carpet. One thinks of lava as something black and ugly. Because of the blended and fused mineral contents, the lavas of the Lassen district are beautifully colored.*

FRONA EUNICE WAIT, 1922

# LASSEN VOLCANIC NATIONAL PARK

**OPPOSITE:** Works Progress Administration poster for the Ranger Naturalist Service in Lassen Volcanic National Park, 1938. It shows Lassen Peak erupting, probably based on the eruptions of 1915–17. On May 22, 1915, one eyewitness recorded: "Terrific eruption. Incomparable with any former eruption . . . column of steam reached 30,000 feet." Those were the only twentieth-century eruptions in the Cascades Volcanic Arc, until Mount St. Helens erupted in 1980.

**ABOVE LEFT:** Daniel Jenks traveled from Rhode Island to California in 1849 in the wake of the discovery of gold at Sutter's Mill. This is one of twenty drawings illustrating his travels that Jenks created after he arrived in Yreka, California, in 1859. He mailed them home to his sister in Pawtucket along with a volume of his edited diary. It is captioned "My Cabin, Long Gulch." Note the open door and window, showing a fireplace and bunk in the single room. There is a woodshed on the left and tools are scattered about the yard.

**ABOVE RIGHT:** Snowplow of the Central Pacific Railroad, near Cisco, California, 1865–69.

AN EXCURSION TO THE BIG TREES OF MARIPOSA *and the Yosemite Valley is not an easy thing. Nevertheless it has become the fashion with the inhabitants of "Frisco." Any man who pretends to be "somebody" either has made this expedition, or announces to his friends that he is about to do so. I have not met many people who have visited these inaccessible regions; but every one tells me he is going—next year. As to roads, there are only tracks; but the railroad which is in process of construction, and which is to unite the mining districts with the main lines, will soon make them superfluous. In the meantime there is a public conveyance, always full of miners, which comes and goes regularly.*

BARON DE HÜBNER, 1871

# YOSEMITE NATIONAL PARK

**PRECEDING PAGES:** View of Yosemite Valley, California, 1899. Note Bridalveil Fall, to the right. The waterfall is 620 feet tall and flows year round. The Ahwahneechee Indians called it *Pohono*, which means *Spirit of the Puffing Wind*. They believed that breathing the mist of the waterfall improved one's chances of getting married.

**TOP LEFT:** The Ahwahnee Hotel, with Half Dome in the background. The hotel, built in 1927, is a classic example of National Park Rustic architecture. It commands a fine view of Yosemite Falls and Glacier Point, as well as Half Dome—all scenic attractions of Yosemite National Park.
**BOTTOM LEFT:** Tobacco label, 1872, showing a view of Yosemite Valley's waterfalls and mountains. The idea, no doubt, was to emphasize the healthfulness and purity of Yosemite tobacco.
**ABOVE:** This 1902 stereoscopic image is captioned: "Our Camp in the Famous Yosemite Valley, near the Yosemite Falls." It shows five people sitting around a table eating and drinking, being served by a sixth. A tent, horses, a wagon, and the falls are visible in the background.
**OPPOSITE:** Photochrom depicting tourists contemplating the view from Glacier Point, including Half Dome, on the left, 1899.

SECURE STAGE SEATS IN ADVANCE. *Take only hand baggage, unless for a protracted visit. For a short trip, an outing suit and two or three waists, with a change for evening wear, will be found sufficient. The free baggage allowance on the stage lines is fifty pounds. . . . Dusters are always advisable, and ladies should provide some light head covering to protect the hair from dust. Sun bonnets are frequently worn. Short skirts are most convenient. Divided skirts are proper for trail trips, as ladies are required to ride astride. Heavy denim for skirt and bloomers is very satisfactory. Such skirts can be hired in the Valley. . . . A soft felt hat is preferable to straw. One that will shade the eyes is best. A cloth traveling cap is the worst thing to wear. Smoked glasses will sometimes save the wearer a headache. . . . A week is the shortest time that should be allowed for a trip to Yosemite. Two weeks are better. The grandeur of the Valley cannot be fully appreciated in a few weeks.*

GALEN CLARK, 1904

## SEQUOIA NATIONAL PARK

OPPOSITE: The base of a redwood tree in Mariposa Grove, a sequoia grove in the southernmost part of Yosemite National Park, near Wawona, California. The grove was discovered in 1857.

ABOVE: The Fallen Monarch is a giant sequoia that fell three hundred years ago; these trees are resistant to decay. Taken in 1911, this picture is a posed tourist photograph of a young boy and girl and their parents. The wagon on the left is dwarfed by the tree.

RIGHT: Stereoscopic view of Wanona, a giant sequoia in Mariposa Grove, sometime after a tunnel was carved through its trunk in 1881. The horse and buggy driving through the tunnel would later be replaced by automobiles. This tree finally toppled in 1969, under the weight of the heavy Pacific winter snow. The tunnel, originally the result of a lightning strike, may have contributed to its collapse. It was 2,300 years old when it fell.

OVERLEAF: The riverboat *J. R. McDonald* ventured up the San Joaquin River as far as Madera, near Fresno, in 1911, in a last attempt to show that the river remained navigable. No riverboat has ventured that far up the river again.

J. R. McDONALD.

*THIS IS A WONDERFUL HARBOR, so large and quiet, with room for so many ships to anchor safely, and such a narrow, well-protected entrance: the Golden Gate. . . . I am perched on the side of Telegraph Hill watching the ships go by. There are twenty-six ships in sight and ten small boats. . . . Just now a British trading ship is going past outward bound, perhaps to be sunk by a German submarine. It is the freight steamers, you know, that they particularly want to get. . . . One sailing ship with dirty-looking sails with clean new patches on them has sailed in and dropped anchor. The sails are running down. Now someone is getting over the side in a little boat. This ship looks like a tramp and I think it is. Little white yachts are scurrying among the larger ships. There are six piers in sight with all kinds of ships tied up to them. One is a British freighter with the flag flying, glad to be safe for awhile I suppose. Another is a Greek ship with several strings of flags flying in the wind. They say that is a sign that it will leave soon. The hills across the bay look beautiful through the fog and Berkeley and Oakland show dimly. The tide is rising now and pouring in through the Golden Gate.*

LAURA INGALLS WILDER, 1915

## SAN FRANCISCO

terrible earthquake razed the first Fairmont. Julia Morgan, who designed William Randolph Hearst's castle at San Simeon, created the majestic grand dame of San Francisco hotels.

**RIGHT:** Baggage label of the Hotel Fairmont.

**BELOW LEFT:** Dining room of the Fairmont in 1907.

**BELOW RIGHT:** Golden Gate Park was built between the 1870s and the 1890s, and the Conservatory (shown here, with the greenhouses) was in place by 1878. It is the oldest conservatory in the western hemisphere.

**OPPOSITE:** New dining room of the Sheraton Palace Hotel, 1980s. The original Palace Hotel, built in 1875, was also totally destroyed by fire in April 1906, in the aftermath of the earthquake, and the New Palace Hotel, renamed Sheraton Palace Hotel in 1954, opened its doors in 1909.

**PRECEDING PAGES:** The Golden Gate Bridge, rising above the mist, with the San Francisco skyline in the distance. The man who dared to bridge the churning waters of the "Golden Gate," the mouth to San Francisco's harbor, was Joseph Strauss, an ambitious but dreamy engineer and poet who had designed for his graduate thesis a 55-mile-long railroad bridge across the Bering Strait.

**ABOVE:** The Fairmont Hotel commands a majestic view in all directions from the top of Nob Hill, where all of San Francisco's cable cars stop. It was built in 1907, just a year after the fires that destroyed much of the city in the wake of the

*[H]ere I am in the very midst of the Chinese quarter. As far as the thick darkness will allow me to judge, the streets are completely deserted. The lower houses are wrapped in sombre shadow. Here and there red paper lanterns swing from balconies, equally painted red, coloured lights glimmer on the wooden pavement, shine through the chinks of the beams, and finally disappear. At every step I stumble against the signboards—long narrow strips of wood, suspended perpendicularly on iron triangles, and blown about by the wind. In some places the darkness is complete, and I can only go on by feeling. In others, momentary and vivid lights, coming from God knows where, creep along the wood-work of the gilt shop shutters and light up some grotesque monster, or the cabalistic red and black letters on one of the signboards.*

BARON DE HÜBNER, 1871

SAN FRANCISCO

ABOVE LEFT, CENTER, AND RIGHT: Street scenes in Chinatown: a public scribe and a basket vendor, photographs from Jules Huret's book *L'Amérique moderne* (1911); two Chinese youths, photochrom, 1902.
RIGHT: Chinese New Year celebrated in San Francisco's Chinatown, as depicted in Jules Huret's book. The Golden Dragon is always featured at the end of the Chinatown New Year's parade, and is greeted with a furious fusillade of firecrackers. The parade has been held regularly since the 1860s.

OPPOSITE: Cable-car traffic proceeding along Market Street, 1911. The unique San Francisco cable-car system runs on the power of massive cables buried beneath the city streets. The car operator pulls a lever that clamps on to the whirring cable and stops the car by releasing the cable. The technology was developed by Andrew Hallidie in the mining fields of the great Gold Rush. It bears a strong resemblance to the technology behind elevators, which makes sense, given the steepness of San Francisco's hills.
OVERLEAF: This photograph of one of the San Francisco wharves in 1894 was taken by Oscar Lange, a leading photographer and occasional landscape painter in the San Francisco Bay area. Steam, fog, and the Pacific sea air combine to create a moving image of a bygone era of sailing ships. That same year, Robert Louis Stevenson died on a Pacific island.

THE ENTIRE SEACOAST OF THIS ISLAND *is cut and worn into caves and as the precipitous and rocky shore line is followed there is a constant series of explosions, the air forcing water violently outward or engulfing it in convulsive swallows to eject it again. The shore is cut into fantastic shapes. At the end of Anacapa Island a fine arch appears, lofty enough for a large vessel to sail under, and not far distant is sighted a mammoth basin, cut out of the rock, and a graceful arch. . . . At Cueva Valdez another remarkable cave is found, worn out by the constant lapping of the Black Current. This is partly on land, its roof extending out over the little bay where its shadow merges into the kelp forest that still follows the shore line. If these caves and the picturesque islands were in the Mediterranean they would be the Mecca of tens of thousands, but being off the coast of California they are rarely visited except by the few.*

WALTER HINES PAGE AND ARTHUR WILSON PAGE, 1902

## SANTA BARBARA CHANNEL ISLANDS

OPPOSITE: This 1901 photochrom shows Franciscan fathers in the garden of the Santa Barbara mission. It was built in 1820, in the aftermath of the great Santa Barbara earthquake, and has remained substantially unchanged to the present day. Its original purpose was to proselytize the Chumash Indians, and it was largely built with Chumash labor.

TOP RIGHT: An 1899 photochrom of Arch Rock on Anacapa Island, one of the Channel Islands off the Ventura County coast. It is now part of the Channel Islands National Park. Arch Rock is a 40-foot-high natural bridge.

BOTTOM RIGHT: Turn-of-the-century photochrom depicting a cluster of California navel oranges.

OVERLEAF, TOP: Panoramic view of Long Beach Pier, south of Los Angeles, 1907. Note the Long Beach Bath House on the left. The mile-long waterfront entertainment and amusement strip was known as The Pike. Long Beach produced some of the most innovative amusement park rides of the early twentieth century.

OVERLEAF, BOTTOM: This view of Long Beach Pier may have been taken from atop the Bath House.

OVERLEAF, INSET: This photograph, taken about 1919 by a photographer credited simply as Evans, shows Myrtle Lind, one of Mack Sennett's Bathing Beauties, posing on the beach with a Graflex single-lens reflex camera. Note the tall leather hood; the photographer looked down to see the viewfinder. Myrtle Lind was successful, and played opposite Oliver Hardy and John Gilbert, but retired from the movies to be married the year this picture was taken. Note the faux sandal straps drawn on her stockings.

Long Beach Pier, Long Beach, Cal. 1907

# MENU

Hors d'Oeuvres Parisienne
Petite Marmite Henri IV
Celery        Salted Almonds        Olives
Brook Trout Saute Fines Herbes
Saddle of Spring Lamb
Fresh String Beans Fleurette
Roman Punch
Filet of Duckling Oregon
Mousseline of Fresh Peas
Potato Souffles
Cold Virginia Ham Glace Mandarin
Salade My Lady
Bombe Victoire
Mignardises
Coffee

I ENTERED THE SUNNY SOUTH HALF A MONTH AGO, *coming down along the cool sea, and landing at Santa Monica. An hour's ride over stretches of bare, brown plain, and through cornfields and orange groves, brought me to the handsome, conceited little town of Los Angeles, where one finds Spanish adobes and Yankee shingles meeting and overlapping in very curious antagonism. I believe there are some fifteen thousand people here, and some of their buildings are rather fine, but the gardens and the sky interested me more. A palm is seen here and there poising its royal crown in the rich light, and the banana, with its magnificent ribbon leaves, producing a marked tropical effect—not semi-tropical, as they are so fond of saying here, while speaking of their fruits. Nothing I have noticed strikes me as semi, save the brusque little bits of civilization with which the wilderness is checkered. These are semi-barbarous or less; everything else in the region has a most exuberant pronounced wholeness.*

JOHN MUIR

## LOS ANGELES

OPPOSITE: Menu from the Los Angeles Biltmore Hotel, which opened in 1923. The name Biltmore is evocative of class and luxury; George Vanderbilt devised it from his own surname for his Asheville estate.

OPPOSITE, INSET: This 1866 patent medicine label for Mercado & Seully California Wine Bitters was produced by a San Francisco company operating from 1862 until about 1870.

ABOVE: Baggage label from the L.A. Biltmore.

TOP RIGHT: A 1940 photograph of the former main entrance of the Biltmore Hotel, on Olive Street, 1940s.

BOTTOM RIGHT: The glamorous Beverly Hills Hotel, early 1950s.

OVERLEAF: Scene from the making of the 1946 Paramount film TWO YEARS *Before the Mast,* starring Alan Ladd, Brian Donlevy, and William Bendix. Hollywood loved making movies set on sailing ships, from *Captain Blood* (with Errol Flynn, 1935) to *Mutiny on the Bounty* (with Marlon Brando, 1962). Entire replica vessels were built. Bosley Crowther, of the *New York Times,* wrote about the making of this movie: "They have chartered a studio square-rigger, on which most of the action takes place, and have given particular attention to the cat-o'-nine-tails and the belaying pins." Note the name of the ship, the *Pilgrim,* on the prow of the dinghy on the right.

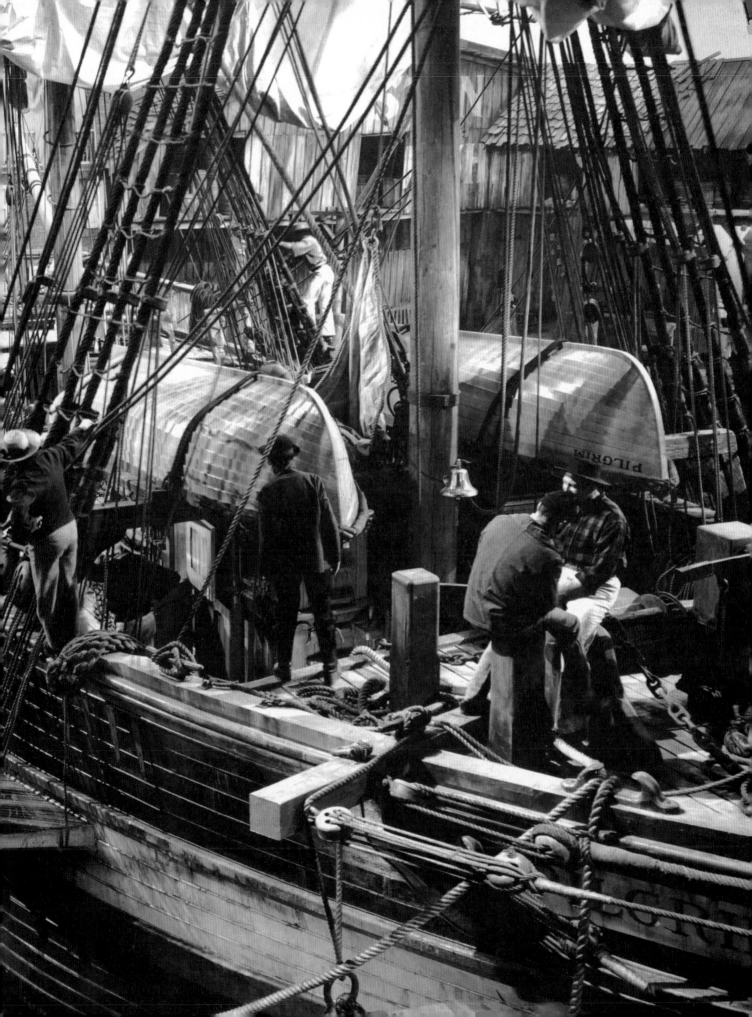

THE PROJECT OF BUILDING AN ELECTRIC AND CABLE ROAD *directly up the face of this great range into the heart of the pine forests that clothe its summits was broached some years since, but there seemed little hope of accomplishing so difficult an undertaking. Finally Prof. T. S. C. Lowe proposed the great cable incline, and by means of his determination and enthusiasm pushed the project to its completion. Today it undoubtedly stands among the great engineering feats of the world, with many novel and daring innovations. Think of it! in less than an hour's ride it is possible to ascend from the orange groves and flower gardens of Pasadena into the heart of the pine forests at an elevation of five thousand feet, where snow covers the ground at times to the depth of many feet. The suddenness of it, the thrilling grandeur of the ride, the rapid changes of scenery and the boundless region over which the eye can sweep make the excursion an event in a lifetime.*

CHARLES AUGUSTUS KEELER, 1899

## LOS ANGELES MOUNT LOWE

**ABOVE AND OPPOSITE:** The Pasadena & Mt. Wilson Railroad Co. ran the Mount Lowe Railway, named after the visionary professor Thaddeus Lowe. The railway ran for just seven years under his ownership, and was devastated by natural and financial disasters of all kinds. The Great Incline, shown here in a 1905 photochrom, was designed by Andrew Hallidie, who created the San Francisco cable-car system.

**OVERLEAF:** Photographer Burton Frasher at Badwater, Death Valley, in 1934. This is the lowest point in the United States, at 282 feet below sea level. The photograph was taken by his son, Burton Frasher, Jr.

**ABOVE:** An 1898 photochrom of a mounted party riding up to Mt. Wilson on Pasadena's Old Trail, the site a few decades later of the spectacular observatory.

**LEFT:** The Los Angeles Alligator Farm was a major city attraction from the year it opened, in 1907, until it moved, almost fifty years later.

BAD WATER
310 FEET
BELOW SEA LEVEL
LOWEST POINT
IN AMERICA
AUTOMOBILE CLUB

*Los Angeles, Cal., Aug. 28 1911—Las Vegas, Nev., has designs on Reno's reputation and prestige as a divorce market, according to information which comes to Los Angeles. Fred Danzig, a Nevada lawyer who knows the divorce law of that State, is said to have begun the building of a big hotel at Las Vegas, and intends to make it especially attractive for a divorce colony. Las Vegas, it is said, will appeal especially for the Winter divorces. As a Winter resort Reno cannot compete with the Southern Nevada town, for the climate of the latter in the cools months is bracing, but not cold, while that of Reno is said to be too chilly for comfort. These are the plans as reported to officials of the Salt Lake Railroad here. The Salt Lake road would profit by having a thriving industry of this kind started at Las Vegas.*

The New York Times, August 29, 1911

LAS VEGAS

**ABOVE:** Las Vegas postcard from the 1940s, depicting the cowboy that would soon thereafter become the 40-foot-tall neon emblem of the city, colloquially known as "Vegas Vic."
**OPPOSITE:** The George Moro Dancers at the El Rancho Vegas Hotel, 1949. The El Rancho Vegas Hotel was the first full-scale casino resort on what would eventually become the Vegas Strip. It opened in 1941.
**OVERLEAF:** Las Vegas in 1988. The dazzling and outsize array of Las Vegas neon, including Vegas Vic, is echoed in the sky by spectacular fireworks.

**TOP:** This silver gelatin photograph shows Las Vegas in 1910, a far cry from its busy present-day appearance.
**ABOVE:** Jazz xylophonist and bandleader Lionel Hampton at the Dunes Hotel in 1956, the year after it opened.

IN AN HOUR OR TWO *the steamer is well in the lea of the island, the rolling is less marked, and the passengers cheer up. They begin to look about for the spout of the California gray whale, exclaim over the splash of a porpoise, and are finally restored to their normal equilibrium by the appearance of a school of flyingfish, skimming over the water with the lightness of a bird. Avalon, in its little half-moon bay, is now plainly visible, and the bold headlands fall off abruptly into the sea. The little town of Avalon, nestled in its sheltered cove, with the mountains rising back of it on all sides and the sea sleeping at its feet, is the only settlement on the island. Along its main street are stores where curiosities, chiefly relating to Western life, are exposed for sale—shells and shell ornaments, Indian baskets, Mexican hats and photographs. The Hotel Metropole, where excellent accommodations may be had, stands out as the most conspicuous structure in the town, while all about are boarding houses, and, during the summer season, a village of tents where thousands of city people live for a happy month or two.*

CHARLES AUGUSTUS KEELER AND LOUISE MAPES BUNNELL KEELER, 1898

## SANTA CATALINA ISLAND

TOP: The 1925 Balboa Bathing Parade, on Balboa Beach in Orange County. The Balboa Pier and the Balboa Pavilion were sister attractions, and every Fourth of July there was a parade of "bathing beauties" in this provincial cousin to the much more glamorous events of Hollywood and Beverly Hills, to the north and northeast, respectively.

OPPOSITE: In 1958 the Four Preps had a nationwide hit with the song that began: "Twenty-six miles across the sea, Santa Catalina is a-waitin' for me." William Wrigley, Jr., founder of the Wrigley's chewing gum empire, developed Santa Catalina Island, building the two-million-dollar Casino Hotel, which stood twelve stories high, making it the tallest structure in Los Angeles County at the time (1929). This 1903 photochrom is of Avalon Bay, well before the Casino was built.

RIGHT: The Hotel Metropole was the first hotel on the island; this photochrom dates from 1901.

251

THE OBJECTIVE POINT, SOONER OR LATER, *of all travelers in this region of the Pacific Coast, is the Hotel del Coronado, which stands unique among the pleasure resorts of America. It is a mammoth frame structure built upon the very brink of the ocean, where the murmur of the waves breaking upon the beach is ever in the air. . . . On approaching the hotel for the first time, the visitor is impressed by its immense size and its freedom from architectural conventions. It is painted white with red roofs, and the lines are so varied and broken by great turrets, spires, towers and dormer windows that it presents a very unique and striking appearance. There surely was never another building constructed on similar lines. With all its seeming irregularity, however, it is built about an immense rectangular court open to the sky and inclosing a beautiful tropical garden. . . . Here rare tropical palms grow to immense size and the air is fragrant with the perfume of the lemon blossom. The California valley quail, in showy plumage and erect helmet crest, runs about here perfectly at home, and humming birds, with their high, fine chatter, dart from blossom to blossom.*

CHARLES AUGUSTUS KEELER AND LOUISE MAPES BUNNELL KEELER, 1898

## SAN DIEGO

PRECEDING PAGES: San Diego's Santa Fe wharf as it appeared in 1910. Manuel Madruga, the dean of San Diego's boat builders, recalled that at the time of this photograph, every Fourth of July the great championship fishing-boat race would be held. Fishing boats would be pulled out of the water and onto the beach and their hulls would be painted with shoe polish to make them faster. As he wrote in 1960: "After the race on Fourth of July, when it got dark, they would tie all the boats together, bow to stern, and would get the Santa Fe tug to pull them around the bay, off the Santa Fe wharf. The boats were all decorated with Chinese lanterns that the city furnished."

TOP LEFT: This train is leaving the newly built Hotel del Coronado, just across San Diego Bay from the city of San Diego, in 1890.

BOTTOM LEFT: Photochrom of a cactus garden in Riverside, California, inland from Los Angeles.

OPPOSITE: View of the magnificent Hotel del Coronado, built in 1888 after the construction of local rail lines. It was the West Coast equivalent of the Ponce de Leon Hotel in St. Augustine, Florida. Among the movies made here, Billy Wilder's *Some Like It Hot* used the Hotel del Coronado as a stand-in for Miami Beach.

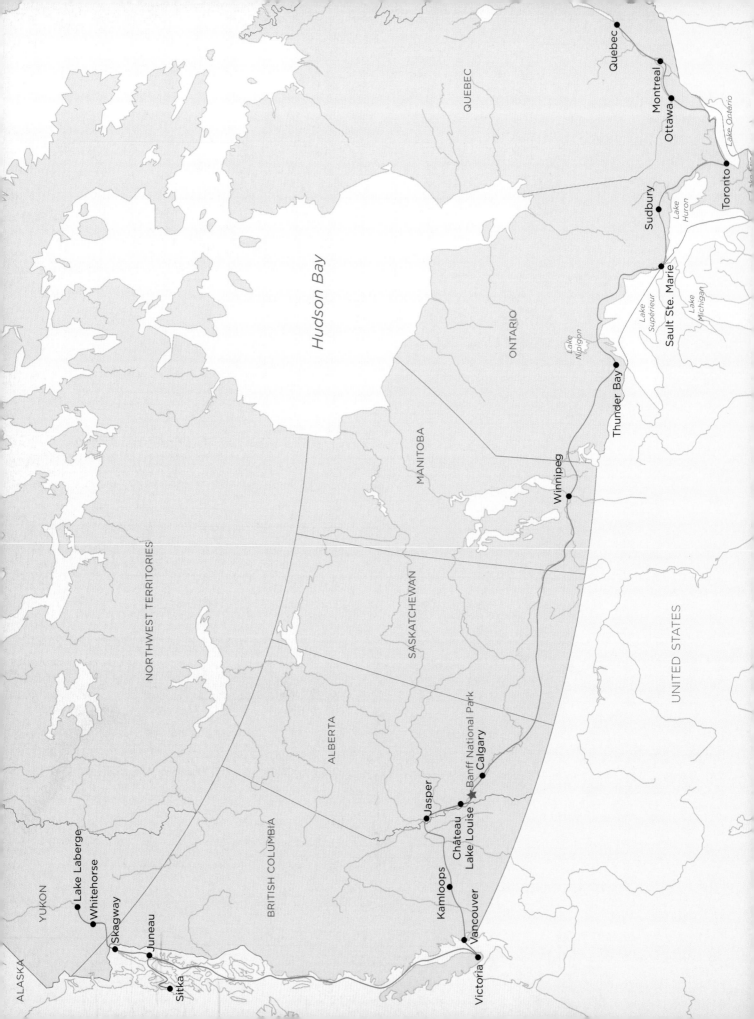

ALASKA

YUKON

Lake Laberge
Whitehorse
Skagway
Juneau

Sitka

NORTHWEST TERRITORIES

BRITISH COLUMBIA

*Hudson Bay*

ALBERTA

SASKATCHEWAN

MANITOBA

QUEBEC

ONTARIO

Lake
Nipigon

Quebec
Montreal
Ottawa
Toronto
Lake Ontario

Sudbury
Sault Ste. Marie
Lake Huron
Lake Michigan

Lake
Supérieur

Thunder Bay

Winnipeg

Calgary
Banff National Park
Château
Lake Louise
Jasper

Kamloops
Vancouver
Victoria

UNITED STATES

"I see, or imagine I see in the future, a race of two million farm-families, ten million people—every farm running down to the water, or at least in sight of it—the best air and drink and sky and scenery of the globe, the sure foundation-nutriment of heroic men and women. The summers, the winters—I have sometimes doubted whether there could be a great race without the hardy influence of winters in due proportion. The honey-bee everywhere; rural ponds and lakes (often abounding with the great white sweet-smelling water-lily); wild fruits and berries everywhere; in the vast flat grounds the prairie anemone. . . . I rose this morning at four and look'd out on the most pure and refulgent starry show. Right over my head, like a Tree-Universe spreading with its orb-apples,—Aldebaran leading the Hyades; Jupiter of amazing lustre, softness, and volume; and, not far behind, heavy Saturn,—both past the meridian; the seven sparkling gems of the Pleiades; the full moon, voluptuous and yellow, and full of radiance, an hour to setting in the west. Everything so fresh, so still; the delicious something there is in early youth, in early dawn—the spirit, the spring, the feel; the air and light, precursors of the untried sun; love, action, forenoon, noon, life—full-fibred, latent with them all."

Thus, in 1880, Walt Whitman described his vision of the Canada of the coming decades. It is lush poetry, but it might just as well have been advertising copy. Many books written in the years that followed for the Canadian Pacific Railway (CPR) resembled these lines by the author of *Leaves of Grass*. Canada was endowed in the same years with its first transcontinental railroad, almost two full decades after the driving of the Golden Spike at Promontory Point in Utah.

Much of the land through which the CPR ran was wilderness. And a substantial chunk of that wilderness was mountainous. Because the most spectacular parts of the Canadian west are the Rockies and the Selkirks (part of a larger range known as the Columbia Mountains), the issue of mountain beauty is an integral part of the story of the settlement and—more to the point—the marketing of the CPR.

In order to appreciate the kind of mental jujitsu involved in marketing mountain wilderness as an attractive vacation spot, it is helpful to read a few excerpts from a book by Sir Leslie Stephen—author, critic, mountaineer, and father of Virginia Woolf and Vanessa Bell. The book is *The Playground of Europe* (a reference to the Alps). In it, Stephen explains how

PRECEDING PAGES: Horseshoe Falls, Niagara, photochrom, 1901.
ABOVE: Château Frontenac (a CPR hotel), Quebec, 1980s.
ABOVE RIGHT: Cover of a CPR brochure, 1928.
RIGHT: The Empress Hotel (a CPR hotel), in the port of Victoria, illustration on the cover of a 1911 brochure for the CPR's Pacific Coast Tours.

the hatred Europeans long felt for mountains had changed over the course of the previous century: "However, in spite of the horrors of eternal snow and prodigious height and steep paths, there are many attractions to be found in the towns; and the wisdom of Providence in forming mountains is justified by certain statistics as to the number of cattle supported on the pasturages and the singular crystals to be found in the rocks. This was indeed a favourite argument at a time when the doctrine of the philosophic Pangloss was so generally popular. Everything must be for the best in this best of all possible worlds, and some final cause must be found even for the Alps. Another contemporary writer, after observing that it is difficult to understand why the Almighty should have raised these 'great excrescences of the earth, which to outward appearance indeed have neither use nor comeliness,' discovers a similar solution of the enigma. Not only are the hideous rocks of the Cevennes, the Vosges, and the Alps 'useful as sending down rivers to the sea, but they are an excellent preserve for fur-bearing animals.' . . . In all the ordinary books we find much the same explanation of the old difficulty. Fur-bearing animals and cheeses and crystals are the missiles with which

ABOVE: Two Sarsi Indians on horseback on the prairies of Alberta, about 1900. Note the tepees in the background, and the blanket in place of a saddle on the horse on the right.
RIGHT: Detail of an ad for Echo Chewing Tobacco, King Buffalo Fine Cut brand, 1873.

vehicle for tourism. Van Horne, having built the railway, began to deck Canada with grand railway hotels.

The hotels are featured on the pages that follow; they range from the Empress in Vancouver to the Royal York in Toronto. In particular, it is the posters advertising the Canadian Pacific Railway that evoke the special magic that the CPR used to bring tourists to Canada. A number of these posters are reproduced here: they clearly show that a strong vision of Canada was at play, ranging from the lovely art advertising the Banff Indian Days to the pastel evocations of Quebec's Château Frontenac in the fall.

Travel across Canada from the east to the west came to its logical conclusion when it reached Vancouver and Victoria. One early Canadian Pacific brochure originally touted its service as "The New Highway to the East." But because by "east" they meant "westward to Asia," in subsequent editions they corrected the brochure's slogan to read: "The New Highway to the Orient."

Confusion over east and west aside, once trains crossing Canada reached the Pacific coast, the passengers could proceed south—or north to Alaska. North to Alaska! became a frenzied cry after the Klondike Gold Rush of 1897. The first 1897 surge northward to the Yukon territory, recounted in the first person by the adventurous Jack London, and a little over a generation later parodied by Charlie Chaplin in his film *The Gold Rush*, was followed at a more leisurely pace by the legendary Harriman Expedition.

Edward Harriman, the railroad tycoon and chairman of the Union Pacific, organized an expedition to Alaska that was memorable both for its luxury and for its scientific ambitions. When the expedition left Seattle on May 31, 1899, it made headlines around the world. Accompanying Harriman on the 9,000-mile voyage along the Alaskan coast was his eight-year-old son Averell and a stunning array of scientists and artists. The names are a who's who of the early conservationist movement: John Muir, the naturalist, author, and advocate of preservation; the great photographer Edward Curtis (two of his photographs from the expedition appear in this book, on pages 306 and 312); the great naturalist and best-selling author John Burroughs; the naturalist George Bird Grinnell (who had turned down an earlier invitation to accompany General Custer on his ill-fated Little Big Horn expedition); and many others.

the unlucky sceptic is overwhelmed, and the ways of Providence satisfactorily vindicated to mankind. . . . That explanation about the fur-bearing animals is so palpably inadequate as to indicate the grievous straits in which the unfortunate reasoner must have found himself confined. Obviously its inventor hated the mountains as a sea-sick traveller hates the ocean, though he may feebly remind himself that it is a good place for the fish."

The discovery that mountains were actually lovely to behold, according to Stephen, was first made on the lakes of Geneva and Constance. By the late nineteenth century, even the "mountainous excrescences" of western Canada were agreed to be places of great beauty, and that was convenient, because the time had come to pay back the investors who had raised the money to build the CPR.

William Cornelius Van Horne was a hard-charging railroad man who had first worked with the notorious James J. Hill, founder of the Minnesota-based Great Northern (who famously, if perhaps apocryphally, said, "Give me snuff, whiskey and Swedes, and I will build a railroad to hell"). He carved out a place for himself in the construction of the CPR, and once the trans-Canadian railway was built, he made it a

On July 31, 1899, the *New York Times* headlined an article on the expedition: "Scientists' Tours in Alaska," continuing with a subhead that ran: "The Harriman Expedition Has Arrived at Seattle, Returning After Many Important Discoveries." Among the findings of the expedition, the article noted: "Many birds and mammals hitherto rare were found in considerable numbers, and it is altogether probable that many new invertebrates are included among the collections made. The geographical results of the expedition are considerable and important." A fjord was named after Mr. Harriman, the article notes, and then adds one more item: "The geologists had many opportunities of studying the rocks and of investigating the action of the glaciers. It was found that most of the glaciers which hitherto have been known and explored are retreating." Well, you can certainly say that again.

The idea of a millionaire outfitting a luxury ship, staffing it with renowned scientists, and sailing into the savage wilderness in pursuit of knowledge is certainly a relic of the vintage era of North American travel. Anyone who has ever watched the original version of King Kong with a skeptical eye is chastened to discover that, at the turn of the century, wealthy industrialists actually set off on this sort of expedition.

In the decades that followed, as the Panama Canal became the preferred way through the continent to the Far East, the overland path west lost its allure. But the coastal route north to Alaska remained an enchanted and privileged thoroughfare to North America's Arctic wilderness.

The Harriman Expedition was a magical distillate of the spirit of vintage travel in North America. Great savants, wealthy industrialists, esteemed artists, all steaming along together, in luxury, daring the elements, discovering a new and astonishing world.

In a sense, then, the story of travel north of the 49th parallel is one of exploration and tourism: whether of railroad tycoons with boats full of artists, scientists, and naturalists, or other railroad tycoons building magnificent hotels in lavish natural settings to bring prosperity to their railways. Of course, there is a second element in the story: the natives whose land these railroad tycoons were so happily colonizing.

It is remarkable that the Harriman expedition was documented by no less a master than Edward Curtis, the great photographer of Native Americans. But Edward Curtis was not present at the 1867 flag lowering (Russian) and flag raising (American) in Sitka that marked the handover of power in what would eventually become the 49th American state.

As it happens, one man who was present at that event (described by a journalist in an eyewitness account on page 312 of this book) had an army career that recapitulates the history of westward expansion. Patrick Ford died at the Soldier's Home in Washington, D.C., in August 1911. His first enlistment was spent fighting the Apaches on the old Santa Fe Trail; during the Civil War he patrolled the offices of General Winfield Scott and was wounded at Antietam. He was then transferred to California and from there to Alaska. He not only raised the Stars and Stripes over "Seward's Folly," as the newly purchased territory was known, but one of his children was the "first white child born in Alaska under the American flag," as the *New York Times* reported it.

ABOVE: Great Northern Railway baggage sticker, 1936.

ABOVE: Sinclair Canyon, along the Banff-Windermere Highway; from an album on the Canadian Rockies, about 1900.
RIGHT: CPR poster to promote travel to Alaska and the Yukon on the Canadian Pacific, undated.

HAVE JUST SEEN SUNRISE *(standing on the extreme bow of the boat), the great round dazzling ball straight ahead over the broad waters,—a rare view. The shores pleasantly, thickly, dotted with houses, the river here wide and looking beautiful in the golden morning's sheen. . . . A pretty shore (miles of it, sitting up high, well-sprinkled with dwellings of habitans [sic],— farmers, fishermen, French cottagers, etc.), verdant everywhere (but no big trees) for fifty miles before coming to Quebec. . . . Approaching Quebec, rocks and rocky banks again, the shores lined for many miles with immense rafts and logs and partially hewn timber, the hills more broken and abrupt, the higher shores crowded with many fine dormer-window'd houses. Sail-ships appear in clusters with their weather-beaten spars and furl'd canvas. . . . Imagine a high rocky hill (the angles each a mile long), flush and bold to the river, with plateau on top, the front handsomely presented to the south and east (we are steaming up the river); on the principal height, still flush with the stream, a vast stone fort, the most conspicuous object in view; the magnificent St. Lawrence itself; many hills and ascents and tall edifices shown at their best— and steeples; the handsome town of Point Levi opposite; a long low sea-steamer just hauling out.*

WALT WHITMAN, 1904

QUEBEC

RIGHT: The Château Frontenac is in the background of this 1960 photograph of an ice skater.
OVERLEAF: Photograph of the toboggan ramps that ran down to the Dufferin Terrace behind the Château Frontenac. The *New York Times* of December 27, 1910, reported, under the headline, "Society at Quebec: Well-Known People There for the Holidays and Winter Sports": "Many Americans are spending the holiday season in Quebec where the attractions of the Winter season are legion. The Chateau toboggan slide on Dufferin Terrace opens this week."

ABOVE: The Terrasse Dufferin, or Dufferin Terrace, under a November snowfall in 1988. This cliff-top promenade offers a magnificent view of the great St. Lawrence River below. Charles Dickens described his visit to Quebec in 1842: "The impression made upon the visitor by this Gibraltar of America: its giddy heights; its citadel suspended, as it were, in the air; its picturesque steep streets and frowning gateways; and the splendid views which burst upon the eye at every turn: is at once unique and lasting." He painted a word-picture of the view from the terrace: "The exquisite expanse of country, rich in field and forest, mountain-height and water, which lies stretched out before the view, with miles of Canadian villages, glancing in long white streaks, like veins along the landscape; the motley crowd of gables, roofs, and chimney tops in the old hilly town immediately at hand; the beautiful St. Lawrence sparkling and flashing in the sunlight."

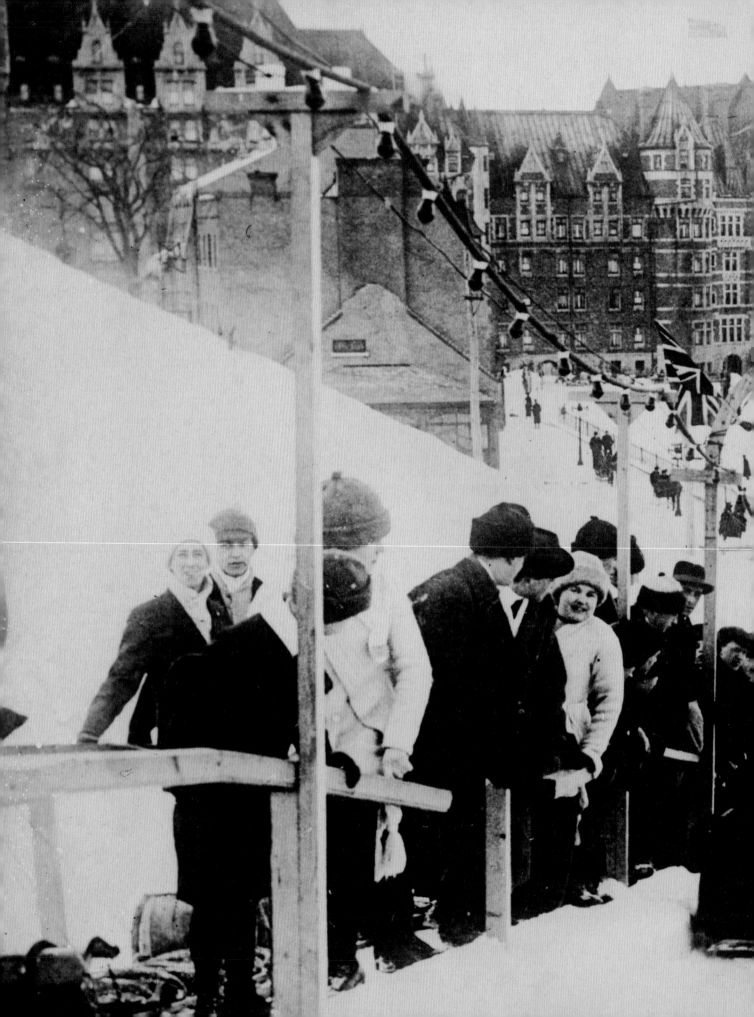

Below Ottawa, on the Quebec side of the river, is Montebello, the seigniory and château of the well-known family of Papineau. The late owner was a son of the noted rebel who led the rising of 1837, and was one of the greatest orators of French Canada. The château, a quaint imitation of a French castle, stands on an eminence close to the river, and is the only example of an old-world edifice of this kind in Canada. The late lord of the manor was only too proud of the part he took in the rebellion, and would show the old musket which he said he had used on that occasion. In his later years he quarrelled with the Roman Church, and became a Protestant, joining the Presbyterian Church and building a fine new church for that body. Sailing further up the river, the voyager arrives at a beautiful part of the country; and soon, at the junction of the Ottawa and the Gatineau, Ottawa comes in sight, the beautiful capital of the Dominion.

SYDNEY ARTHUR FISHER, GEORGE JOHNSON, 1905

## MONTEBELLO
## OTTAWA VALLEY

**TOP LEFT:** The spectacular lounge of Le Château Montebello, a resort hotel originally known as the Seigniory Club. The centerpiece of this spectacular wooden structure is what is described in the hand-lettered caption on this photograph as the "six-hearthed fireplace chimney," a central stone pier rising seventy feet into the air, supporting the sixty-foot log beams of the rotunda's roof.

The hotel, built in just four months in 1930, still stands, and is now the property of the Fairmont Corporation, the accommodations branch of the Canadian Pacific Railway. When the CPR purchased the Seigniory Club in 1970, it changed its name to Le Château Montebello, in part to identify it with its overall tradition of "château" hotels. Others have described the magnificent building differently: never one to mince words, Margaret Thatcher called it the world's largest log cabin.

There are dark stories behind the painted-black-log structure that overlooks the Ottawa River valley. One involves an owner of the Montebello estate that now adjoins Le Château Montebello: Louis-Joseph Papineau, whose home, Monte-Bello, is at the center of the Manoir-Papineau National Historic Site of Canada. Papineau was a prominent supporter of autonomy for the French-speaking province of Quebec, and his role in the 1837 rebellion against British rule forced him into exile until he was pardoned by Queen Victoria.

**BOTTOM LEFT:** An elegant client of the Seigniory Club is fitted for skis in 1940.

**OPPOSITE:** Guests sunning amid deep snow at the Seigniory Club in 1940. Among the guests in the gala years were show-business royalty—Bing Crosby, Perry Como, Bette Davis, and Joan Crawford—and actual royalty—Japan's Crown Prince Akihito, Princess Juliana of the Netherlands, Prince Rainier and Princess Grace of Monaco, and the Duke of Windsor, both before and after his abdication.

*Six-hearthed Fireplace Chimney and Main Lounge, Log Lodge.*

THREE HOURS ON MOUNT ROYAL, *the great hill and park back of Montreal; spent the forenoon in a leisurely most pleasant drive on and about the hill; many views of the city below; the waters of the St. Lawrence in the clear air; the Adirondacks fifty miles or more distant; the excellent roads, miles of them, up hill and down; the plentiful woods, oak, pine, hickory; the French signboards —Passez a droite—as we zigzag around; the splendid views, distances, waters, mountains, vistas, some of them quite unsurpassable; the continual surprises of fine trees, in groups or singly; the grand rocky natural escarpments; frequently open spaces, larger or smaller, with patches of goldenrod or white yarrow, or along the road the red fire-weed or Scotch thistle in bloom; just the great hill itself, with its rocks and trees unmolested by any impertinence of ornamentation.*

WALT WHITMAN, 1880

MONTREAL

The Terrace at the Look-Out, Mount Royal, Montreal

1900. This is one of two belvederes in Mount Royal Park, overlooking the city from atop a hill whose highest peak rises about 750 feet. The first European to climb Mount Royal—in French, Mont-Royal—was Jacques Cartier in 1535. At the time, Canada was French, and France still had royalty.

**OPPOSITE:** Another creation of the Canadian Pacific Railway, the Place Viger Hotel was designed by Bruce Price, who was also the architect of the CPR Château Frontenac and the CPR Banff Springs Hotel (the wooden version, which burned down in 1926). The Place Viger Hotel contained the railway station on its lower levels; the upper levels housed a luxurious and elegant hotel. The development of Montreal was not kind to the Place Viger; the hotel closed in 1935 and the railway station was shut down in 1951. The city bought the building, gutted it, and turned it into drab office space.

**PRECEDING PAGES:** Place Jacques-Cartier, in Old Montreal, as shown in a photochrom by William Henry Jackson, 1900. The view is of the square on Market Day. In the distance is a column with a statue of Lord Horatio Nelson, erected in Montreal in 1808 by the English merchants of the city 33 years before the column in Trafalgar Square, London.

**ABOVE LEFT:** This is half of a two-image stereoscopic view of a castle made of blocks of ice; note the children with a toboggan in the foreground and the horse-drawn sleigh on the right. Montreal pioneered the construction of ice castles and ice palaces; St. Paul, Minnesota, was the first location in the United States to take up the tradition (in the late 1880s), and it soon spread to upstate New York and Colorado. The *Montreal Witness* of January 5, 1889, reported that 50 men were at work on the ice palace that year before a "large crowd of spectators."

**ABOVE RIGHT:** The Kondiaronk Belvdere, shown in a postcard from

# Canadian Pacific Hotels

## from ATLANTIC to PACIFIC

A Typical Lodge

Hotel Saskatchewan, Regina

The Pines, Digby, N.S.

Chateau Frontenac, Quebec, Que.

Algonquin Hotel, St. Andrews, N.B.

Royal York Hotel, Toronto, Ont.

Royal Alexandra Hotel, Winnipeg, Man.

Lakeside Inn, Yarmouth, N.S.

Cornwallis Inn, Kentville, N.S.

Chateau Lake Louise, Lake Louise, Alta.

Hotel Palliser, Calgary, Alta.

Banff Springs Hotel, Banff, Alta.

Operated by the Vancouver Hotel Co. Ltd. on behalf of the C.P.R. and C.N.R.

Hotel Vancouver, Vancouver B.C.

Emerald Lake Chalet, Emerald Lake (near Field, B.C.)

Empress Hotel, Victoria, B.C.

CANADIAN PACIFIC HOTELS

WORLD'S GREATEST TRAVEL SYSTEM

*Ottawa is a little city, a compromise capital, created to steer a middle course between the rival claims of Montreal and Toronto. It is almost equally French and English, Catholic and Protestant; and when the tide of official life slackens, it is still kept busy by its important lumber trade. The country-side is one of even more than usually lovely rivers. If water, as I am inclined to think, is the loveliest thing in Nature, then Canada must be as rich in beauty as any country upon earth. The Lièvre, the Gatineau, the Rideau, the great Ottawa itself; as power reserves and waterways essential as they are beautiful. ... We had a welcome if a fleeting taste of official Canada; we introduced the savage joys of the picnic into the stately routine of Staff life; we dug for fossils in the deep grey clay of the Ottawa's bed; we attended a race-meeting; assisted at the entertainment of a party of British journalists; visited the Parliament Buildings and the Archives; explored the National Gallery; feasted, talked and enjoyed, unreproved, all the inquisitive privileges of middle age!*

YVONNE FITZROY, 1929

## OTTAWA

DE LA FENÊTRE DU WAGON
CANADIAN NATIONAL RAILWAYS

le CANADA

a brochure of
Toronto, 1938.
acdonald also
katchewan in
Regina. The
an Pacific
us Van Horne,
agnificent
bring
He famously
xport the
tourists."
te, in
e Bay of
Ontario, 1913.

ABOVE RIGHT: Parliament Hill and the Parliament Buildings, Ottawa, 1900. Ottawa became the capital of Canada in 1858. Although it was an undistinguished industrial town, it had two features to recommend it: it was at a "safe" distance from the United States, and it stood midway between the Atlantic and the Pacific.

LEFT: The Lord Elgin Hotel in downtown Ottawa was built in 1941. It was named in honor of James Bruce, 8th Earl of Elgin, and first governor of the united Canadas.

FACSIMILE: Brochure in French for the Canadian Pacific Railway, 1930s. Note in particular the multilingual blend of: "Rodeos de Cowboys."

AT FIRST WE SPED ON OUR WAY, *but later it was not only quite easy to believe that a third of the population of Canada lived in South Ontario; rather it was difficult not to believe that the whole nine million resided on wheels on the Kingston-Toronto road. The cars passed in one long stream. . . . As you approach the city sudden, deep valleys carry your eye to the blue sea of the lake. The opposite shore is invisible, and the smoke of big steamers stains the horizon. . . . . We spent a long afternoon at the Museum, which is said by many to possess the finest Chinese collection in existence. It was on this collection that I concentrated, though I was led astray for some exciting minutes by a little screen hung with Moghul miniatures. We were both led astray by the gown worn by Queen Mary at the State Entry into Delhi, which made us more than ever reverent of royal endurance! We saw Queen Victoria's "house" shoes—and a dear little, tiny pair that had belonged to Mary Stuart. There is something appealingly intimate about shoes, especially fragile shoes, made for fragile, exquisite people.*

YVONNE FITZROY, 1929

TORONTO

ABOVE: Dining room of the Royal York Hotel in Toronto, sometime in the 1950s or 1960s. The waiter in the lower left corner of the photograph is eyeing the camera with some concern, immortalized in that pose.

BOTTOM LEFT: Brochure of the Royal York Hotel, 1938. Completed in 1929, it stood 28 stories tall, making it the tallest building in Toronto. It was for many years the largest hotel in the British Empire, as the brochure notes. It boasted ten elevators and a private shower or bath, as well as a radio in each of its 1,048 rooms. It was one of the flagship hotels of the Canadian Pacific Railway, and it stood across the street from Toronto's Union Station. It is still a major Toronto hotel, and Queen Elizabeth takes an entire floor here for her entourage when she is in Toronto.

OPPOSITE: Entrance to the Royal York Hotel, 1930. The interior features magnificent hand-painted ceilings, travertine pillars, ornate furnishings, crystal chandeliers, and wall hangings.

*Winnipeg will hold its own with any hustling point in America. It is a "live city"; about that there can be no mistake. We had scarcely emerged from the station buildings when copies were distributed to us of the "Manitoba First Primer," a brochure comical, statistical, and pictorial, illustrative of the industries of the province and their rapid growth in recent years. From the primer I learned that Manitoba is a corruption of two Indian words, Manitou Wapa, "God's Country"; and I hope to show that not without good reason has the Indian appellation been retained. . . . One is not surprised at finding in the outskirts of cities as populous as Montreal and Toronto mansions evidently the residences of men with large incomes. When, however, we come to cities with populations under fifty thousand, the number of such residences excites the Englishman's wonder, as the impression is conveyed of whole communities revelling in opulence. The astonishment is not lessened when one takes into account the cost of building, the high wages of skilled labour, and the enormity of rents for house property in Western Canada.*

JAMES LUMSDEN, 1903

# FORT WILLIAM
# BRANDON
# WINNIPEG

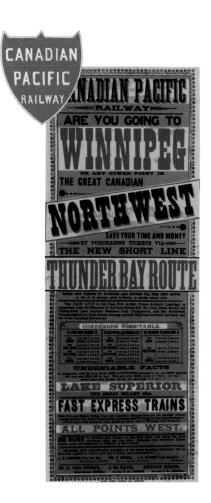

*C.P.R. Yards and Depot, Brandon, Man.*

PRECEDING PAGES: Interior of a bungalow on the Nipigon River in Ontario, 1920s. The river drains Lake Nipigon into Lake Superior, with a total drop of 250 feet over thirty miles. The river is legendary for the size of the brook trout caught there. In the aftermath of World War I, the Canadian Pacific Railway established more affordable accommodations in this area, in the form of bungalow camps.

OPPOSITE: A pair of wooden snowshoes on display at the Fort William Historical Park (formerly known as Old Fort William) in Thunder Bay, Ontario. The park is a historical replica of Fort William as it existed in 1815. The original fort was destroyed long ago, buried under CPR railway tracks and coal piles in the 1880s. The historical park features reconstructed buildings and costumed historical interpreters.

ABOVE: Canadian Pacific Railway Yards and Depot in Brandon, Manitoba, postcard, 1908. Nicknamed the Wheat City, Brandon is the second-largest city in Manitoba, after Winnipeg. This view of the railway station (built in 1887) was taken from the Eighth Street bridge. The west-bound train is seen on the left side; east-bound on the right. The tall building in the background on the right was the Brandon Brewing Company. On the left side behind the smoke from the steam engine was the Maple Leaf Milling Company's grain elevator and flour mill.

LEFT: This 1883 timetable for the Canadian Pacific Railway offers schedules for Winnipeg via the Thunder Bay Route and information about a number of steamer lines on Lake Superior.

INSET: Canadian Pacific Railway baggage sticker.

A CANADIAN PACIFIC HOTEL
HOTEL PALLISER
COFFEE SHOP AT POPULAR PRICES..

AT THREE O'CLOCK NEXT MORNING, *Christian called me and I got up . . . and then went out to breakfast by firelight, . . . At four o'clock we three started. We went up a very steep snow-slope, which required some step-cutting, as the snow was so hard, and near the top there was a good deal of danger from falling stones. . . . Some of the rocks were covered with ice, which made climbing very difficult, but on our descent the sun had turned the ice to water, and we got several shower-baths. . . . When near the ridge, we found the remains of a mountain-rat or some small animal, with teeth and claws and fur still good, which had evidently been dropped by some large bird, as no animal could have lived up there. We reached the summit at two p.m. but though the day was cloudless there was too much smoke from forest-fires, in the horizon, to get a very distant view. The summit was much corniced, so we gave it a wide berth, and after a short stay began the descent. [Editorial Note. Miss Gertrude E. Benham's modest and unassuming account of her ascent of Mt. Assiniboine would not lead the reader to suppose that she was the first and only lady to set foot upon its summit, 11,880 feet above the sea.]*

GERTRUDE E. BENHAM, 1907

## CANADIAN ROCKIES

PRECEDING PAGES: Billboard advertising the Palliser Hotel, Calgary, Alberta, 1940. The Palliser opened in 1914. It was named after Captain John Palliser, an Irish explorer whose work in the region in the mid-nineteenth century resulted in the dissolution of the monopoly of the Hudson Bay Company. The building was designed in the Chicago School style.

OPPOSITE: Mt. Assiniboine, often dubbed the Matterhorn of the Canadian Rockies (because of its similarity in shape to the Swiss peak), photographed by noted mountain photographer Byron Harmon, 1924.

TOP RIGHT: Photo album illustrating the Canadian Rockies. The cover illustration depicts Lake Louise, Alberta, c. 1900.

BOTTOM RIGHT: Special Canadian Pacific Railway train, complete with darkroom, for William McFarlane Notman, a distinguished photographer who had done a photographic expedition for the CPR in 1884. That expedition was so successful that the CPR provided him with this train for his subsequent expeditions in 1887 and 1889.

INSET: Canceled postage stamps from Victoria, British Columbia.

*WE ARE NOW IN THE MIDST OF SCENES which, to do them justice, would require some one accustomed to word painting of the highest order, such, indeed, as Lady Macdonald, who has written very beautifully and expressively concerning them, but her remarks are so well known that it will be needless to repeat them. So extremely varied are the scenes which continually rise to view in these regions, so clear the air, and so cut up, distorted, hacked, haggled, wriggled, and precipiced in every conceivable way are the mountains, and so fascinatingly beautiful at every turn are their surroundings as well as themselves, that for hours together I have stood on the platform of the cars drinking in those scenes of loveliness in such a manner as to enable me now, as they rise before me, to write about them as I found them. More than this, with the object of accomplishing my ends as fully as possible, I obtained the kind permission of the Company to ride on their locomotives over any part of the country I pleased. Returning to Banff, I . . . found myself in the midst of landscapes of rare beauty and sublimity of which I cannot say too much.*

JOHN WILTON CUNINGHAME HALDANE, 1908

BANFF

PRECEDING PAGES: Aerial view of the Banff Springs Hotel, as it was rebuilt following the fire in 1926.

ABOVE LEFT: Lobby of the first Banff Springs Hotel, completed in 1888. It was the second in the chain of magnificent railway hotels envisioned by tycoon William Cornelius Van Horne. It was built in the Scottish Baronial style, and made entirely of wood. The wood in the lobby was varnished red pine. This photograph dates to the 1890s.

ABOVE RIGHT: Poster for the Banff Indian Days, 1930s. Promoted with the assistance of the Canadian Pacific Railway, the Banff Indian Days began in 1889. When a CPR train was blocked in Banff by a rockslide, the CPR manager contacted the local Stoney tribe and asked them if they could come entertain the stranded passengers. The one-time event became a regular thing, held annually until the late 1970s. They were resumed in 2004.

OPPOSITE: The CPR hired Swiss guides to accompany vacationers in the mountains around the original Banff Springs Hotel (seen in the background, before the fire that destroyed it in 1926).

OVERLEAF: View of the Bow River from a room in the Banff Springs Hotel, November 1988. The Bow River flows southeast from the Bow Glacier through Lake Louise, Banff, and Calgary before merging into the Saskatchewan River and, ultimately, into Lake Winnipeg and Hudson Bay.

BEFORE LEAVING BANFF *I bought a store of currant buns for a certain and, I feared, a wholly legendary bear that had been know to "hold-up" the passing motorist. The snow was creeping down the mountain-sides, powdering the forests, the rain fell in a cold drizzle, and any animal, I felt, fortunate enough to possess the hibernating habit must sure be tucked up. Yet the general greyness could not dim the golden poplars which shone by the roadside, driving back the spruce and pine, and even climbing higher than these, far up the mountain walls. We followed the river valley, driving cautiously on a greasy surface, till, by the middle of the morning, depressed by surrounding gloom and chill, our thoughts turned longingly to buns! We had started early; the world was very comfortless; bears, after all, but creatures of legend; and the buns were actual and superb. Yet we stifled the pangs of hunger, rounded a curve, and there—shambling down the road towards us—he came, a perfectly real black bear. Suddenly the solitude seemed very solitary, and bears not perhaps the mildest members of the brute creation. But heroically K. slowed up while I dived for the paper bag. Bun number one was snatched from her hand, bun number two we threw after it in hasty propitiation.*

YVONNE FITZROY, 1929

## LAKE LOUISE

OPPOSITE: Canadian Pacific Railway promotional photograph for the Chateau Lake Louise, 1930s.

ABOVE LEFT: Poster advertising the Chateau Lake Louise, 1938. The magnificent illustration is the work of Alfred Crocker Leighton. Leighton was a young architecture student, born in 1901, who lied about his age to get into the Royal Flying Corps in World War I. He was badly injured,

but recovered. He built a working scale model of the port of Liverpool, which brought him to the attention of the Canadian Pacific Railway. He was responsible for the founding of the Banff School of Fine Arts.

ABOVE RIGHT: Lake Louise was discovered in 1882, and was named after Queen Victoria's fourth daughter, Princess Louise Caroline Alberta, who was married to John

Campbell, the governor general of Canada at the time (the province of Alberta was also named after her). The lake has a lovely emerald color, from the ground "rock flour" carried into the water by meltwater from glaciers. Originally a "chalet," but upgraded in time to a "chateau," it is one of the grand railway hotels built by the Canadian Pacific Railway.

ABOUT HALF WAY DOWN THE HILL *a beautiful valley opens out, formed by the north fork of the Kicking Horse River; blue woods recede into purple forests, and these again swell into an amphitheatre of lofty mountains, whose peaks had caught and held the first rays of sunlight, and were glowing in rainbow lines, while all below was mist and shadow. Soon the bottom of the descent was reached, where the river, increased by the streams running into it, widens into a broad shallow bed more than half clay, and spreads itself over it in several channels, fordable at Field, where we paused for breakfast. There was no dining car attached to the train (it had been dispensed with the preceding night, after supper, to avoid carrying its weight down the Kicking Horse Pass, and another car was to be attached for dinner).*

MRS ARTHUR SPRAGGE, 1887

## YOHO NATIONAL PARK

**LEFT:** This 1902 photochrom depicts Emerald Lake and the Van Horne Range in British Columbia. The oldest range in the Canadian Rockies, it is part of the Yoho reserve, now a Canadian national park. The Kicking Horse River originates in ice fields in the park, and has cut a spectacular natural bridge through the rock. The Burgess Shale, discovered in 1909 by Charles Doolittle Walcott, a secretary of the Smithsonian Institution, is one of the world's richest fossil troves. The Cree Indians are said to have stopped short in awe and wonder at the sight of this landscape and cried, "Yoho!"

**OPPOSITE:** Twin Falls, in Yoho National Park, are segmented by a massive stone block, and catapult down almost 600 feet. At the foot of the falls is the Twin Falls Chalet, built in 1908 by the Canadian Pacific Railway. Some people joke that the proper name of the Rocky Mountains of Canada is the Canadian Pacific Rockies, so ubiquitous is the name of the CPR.

**PRECEDING PAGES:** Mount Stephen and at its foot, on the banks of the Kicking Horse River, the Mount Stephen House, named after a president of the CPR. The nearby town of Field, refreshingly, was named after Cyrus West Field, who laid the first transatlantic telegraph cable, and had nothing to do with the CPR.

# SELKIRK MOUNTAINS

ABOVE: This photochrom was published in 1902, by the Detroit Photographic Company. It was based on a black-and-white glass-plate transparency that formed part of a four-image panorama (one section of which has since been lost). Although there is no attribution, it is reasonable to suspect that this photograph was taken by Henry G. Peabody during his visit to the Selkirks. Mount Sir Donald was originally named Syndicate Peak in honor of the group who arranged the financing for the Canadian Pacific Railway, but the name was changed to honor the leader of that syndicate, Sir Donald

Alexander Smith, 1st Baron Strathcona and Mount Royal.
LEFT: This promotional brochure was published by the CPR in the 1890s. An earlier version of the brochure trumpeted: "The Canadian Pacific: The new highway to the East across the mountains, prairies, and rivers of Canada." The wording was amended from "the East" to "the Orient," because of the evident confusion: the railway ran west to the Pacific. The bridge pictured here, the steel-truss Stoney Creek Bridge, was built in 1893 and rises 300 feet above the valley floor. It is something like a corporate emblem of the CPR.

OPPOSITE: The caption for this hand-tinted photograph by Henry G. Peabody, published by the Detroit Photographic Company around 1902, reads: "Crevasse formation in Illecillewaet Glacier, Selkirk Mountains, British Columbia, Canada." Peabody (1855–1951) was a prolific photographer who traveled the country and ran studios in both Boston and Pasadena. He worked with companies and organizations ranging from the National Geographic Society to the Encyclopaedia Britannica and the Atchison, Topeka, and Santa Fe Railway. He also held lectures and organized "lantern slide" projections.

I STOPPED OFF OVER SUNDAY AND MONDAY AT GLACIER, *a wild and romantic spot in the Selkirk Mountains. It is an ideal spot for the lover of mountains and of mountain climbing. The altitude is 4122 feet. The Illecillewaet River plunges and roars down the steep valley, white with glacier milk. . . . Before breakfast the next morning I walked through the woods, a mile and a half up the mountain stream, to the foot of the great Illecillewaet Glacier. . . . And then I came to a wall, a huge mass, an upward stretching field, of ice, dingy and dirty without, but beautifully green within, as seen in the crevices and caves. From beneath it flowed a good-sized milky stream, the milky color being caused by the glacial flour, or finely ground rock. Down the sides were gliding rills of pure ice-water. Stones and piles of dirt, embedded in the ice or borne on its surface, were gradually nearing the end of their journey, a journey of a mile perhaps in space, but of very many years in time. What a new birth it must be to the ice, that has been moving perhaps one foot a day, when it turns into water and speeds away in the brook many miles in an hour! On the under side of the glacier I saw tunnels of different sizes and lengths. They were of the same diameter and shape as the stones I saw at their upper ends. The stones were caught fast in the ground and the glacier had ploughed its way over and around them, or rather it had flowed around them without any breaking of the ice. The glacier observes the same law of motion that water does in flowing, the law of fluids in motion.*

ROSELLE THEODORE CROSS, 1921

AT ONE O'CLOCK WE REACHED THE GLACIER HOTEL, *close to the station of that name, three miles west of the summit of the Selkirks. It is a most artistic building, somewhat of the Swiss chalet style, built by the enterprise of the C. P. R. Co. and intended as a summer resort for many who will now be enabled for the first time to enjoy genuine Canadian mountain air. No more lovely spot could have been selected for its situation, commanding as it does a veritable, though much disputed, sea of mountains of the grandest description; the peaks of those above-mentioned [Mount Carroll, Mount Sir Donald, and Mount Hermit] are all in view, while not a mile from the hotel lies a large glacier, a sea of green, glittering ice. There were both bear and elk close to the hotel last summer, an attraction to sportsmen in search of big game.*

MRS ARTHUR SPRAGGE, 1887

## GLACIER

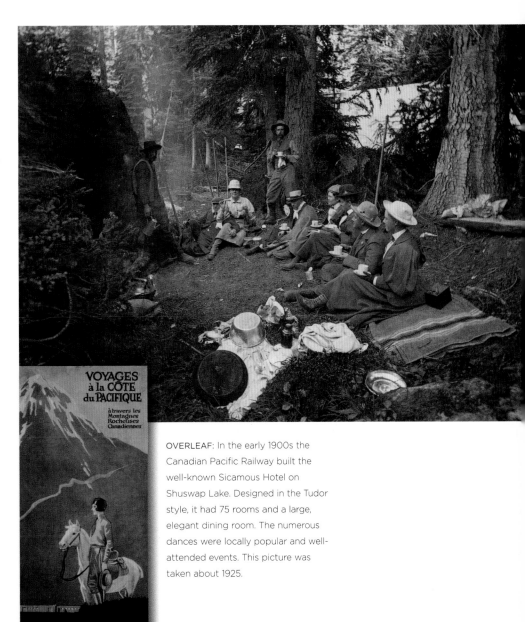

OPPOSITE: William McFarlane Notman took this glass-plate photograph of the Illecillewaet Glacier and the new station at Glacier, British Columbia, in 1887.

TOP RIGHT: Excursion and picnic in the vicinity of the Glacier House (a Canadian Pacific Railway dining station inaugurated in 1887); a Vaux (pron. like "fox") family photograph, c. 1900. Seated, center, in white, is Mary Vaux Walcott, a member of the prominent Philadelphia Vaux family and wife of Charles D. Walcott, a director of the Smithsonian Institution. Born in 1860, she was a tireless painter of North American plants, an accomplished mountaineer, a photographer, and a pioneer in the study of glaciers. A mountain in the Canadian Rockies—Mt. Mary Vaux— was named after her. She said of the Canadian Rockies, "Nowhere else is there such a wealth of beauty and interest, and I conclude that the haunts so attractive to the world have no attraction for me."
BOTTOM RIGHT: CPR brochure, c. 1925.

OVERLEAF: In the early 1900s the Canadian Pacific Railway built the well-known Sicamous Hotel on Shuswap Lake. Designed in the Tudor style, it had 75 rooms and a large, elegant dining room. The numerous dances were locally popular and well-attended events. This picture was taken about 1925.

Chasse. — Parmi le gros gibier canadien, il faut compter l'Orignal, l'Ours gris, le Mouflon, la Chèvre-Antilope, le Caribou, quatre variétés de Cerfs.

Le Caribou.

L'Orignal.

Le Mouflon.

I MUST NOT LINGER OVER THE LAST THIRTY MILES OF RAIL TO VANCOUVER AND THE COAST. . . . *For the last dozen miles or so the track follows the winding shores of Burrard inlet, till it gradually widens into Vancouver Harbour. It is all very beautiful. The densely-wooded mountains of the coast range, snow-capped by November and often earlier, rise into the sky, while the leafy slopes and promontories of their foothills reflect their gorgeous colouring in the narrow waters of the fiord. . . . And as one runs slowly into Vancouver and sees the busy city covering the slopes beside the water, the big ships and liners lying off it in the most beautiful harbour in the world, one tries to realise that twenty years ago this whole scene was an obscure wilderness of wood and water. The transformation is, of course, due to the fact of the Canadian Pacific Railway having made its terminus here. In 1885 it reached Port Moody, and two years later was extended to Vancouver City, which had built itself up and already been burned to the ground, only to be restored on a greater scale before the first train steamed into it.*

ARTHUR GRANVILLE BRADLEY, 1905

## VANCOUVER
## VICTORIA

**OPPOSITE, TOP:** Waterfront Station, Vancouver, British Columbia, built by the Canadian Pacific Railway in 1910, the Pacific terminus for transcontinental trains.
**OPPOSITE, CENTER:** Double page of illustrations from a Canadian National Railways brochure, 1930s.
**OPPOSITE, INSET:** Stanley Park is a 1,000-acre urban park, established in 1888, and covered with huge Douglas fir, Western Red cedar, Western Hemlock, and Sitka Spruce trees.
**ABOVE:** The Empress Hotel, in Victoria, is a chateau-style hotel (built in 1904–8, with two wings added in 1909–14; seen here c. 1930) modeled on the Château Frontenac, which it bookends on the Pacific Coast. The Empress is a lovely hotel, but the life of its architect is even more compelling than the hotel he built. It was the work of Francis Mawson Rattenbury, an English-born architect who worked for the Canadian Pacific Railway as the Western Division Architect. Rattenbury broke off ties with the CPR and went to work for their competition, the Grand Trunk Pacific Railway. He designed many hotels and stations for the GTP, but none was completed after the president, Charles Melville Hays, went down with the *Titanic*. The company subsequently went bankrupt. At age 68 Rattenbury was murdered by his 27-year-old second wife's 18-year-old lover.

## TAKU GLACIER

PRECEDING PAGES: The U.S.R.C. *Bear* and the S.S. *Corwin*, a revenue cutter and a coast guard ship, respectively. Photograph of unknown date. Note the figurehead of a polar bear just below the bowsprit. The *Corwin* was sent on a rescue mission in 1881 that was immortalized by John Muir in his book *The Cruise of the Corwin.* The *Bear* was sent to rescue the Greely mission in 1884, after a terrible winter in which 19 of the 25 men in the expedition died. There were rumors of cannibalism.

ABOVE: Glaciers in Taku Inlet, 1914. This young man appears to be pretending to pay gallant court to a block of ice that distantly resembles a woman. The caption reads: "Flirting in Alaska."

LEFT: Icebergs, bay, and mountain in background, Alaska, by Edward S. Curtis. A renowned photographer whose portraits of Native Americans are highly regarded, Curtis traveled to Alaska in 1899 with a crew that included railroad tycoon E. H. Harriman, his son Averell, conservationist John Muir, prominent scientist C. Hart Merriam, and nature writer John Burroughs.

[T]HE TAKU GLACIER . . . *has size and something more. It is some seventy-five miles long, and on its face wall where it breaks into the sea it must be three-quarters of a mile in breadth and probably several hundred feet in height. If the Palisades of the Hudson, where they break abruptly to the river, were a little smaller and made up of ice they would look not unlike the front of this glacier. The up-and-down structure of the Palisades rock is similar to the ice formation of the glacier save that the latter is finer, more flaky, more crystalline. Imposing and beautiful as this ice structure is in form, the beauty of the coloring goes far beyond all else. One never sees, in any of the mountain glaciers of the temperate zone, such wonderful blues and greens as those in the Alaskan glaciers. The hue is exquisite, jewel-like, and in depth unsurpassed. Even when the ice breaks off in huge blocks and slowly floats away as a small iceberg the splendid color goes with it and is reflected in the water. The Alaskan glaciers (they are only the southern tongues of the great arctic ice-cap) are not mere matters of wonder, they are things of beauty. The great ones, like the Muir, the Pacific, and the Valdez Glaciers— the latter with fifteen miles of frontal ice-cliffs—have an even greater beauty of color than those more accessible.*

JOHN CHARLES VAN DYKE, 1916

THEY TURNED AND TWISTED, *now crossing the river, now coming back again, sometimes making half a dozen attempts before they found a way over a particularly bad stretch. It was slow work. . . . There were days when they made fifteen miles, and days when they made a dozen. And there was one bad stretch where in two days they covered nine miles, being compelled to turn their backs three times on the river and to portage sled and outfit over the mountains. At last they cleared the dread Fifty Mile River and came out on Lake Le Barge [sic]. Here was no open water nor jammed ice. For thirty miles or more the snow lay level as a table; withal it lay three feet deep and was soft as flour. Three miles an hour was the best they could make, but Daylight celebrated the passing of the Fifty Mile by traveling late. At eleven in the morning they emerged at the foot of the lake. . . . At eight in the evening they left the lake behind and entered the mouth of the Lewes River. Here a halt of half an hour was made, while chunks of frozen boiled beans were thawed and the dogs were given an extra ration of fish.*

JACK LONDON, 1915

## DAWSON CITY
## LAKE LABERGE

ABOVE: Loading equipment and dogs to travel up the Yukon River in December 1897. Jack London had made this same journey three months earlier. He described the Yukon River as "a dangerous crossing of lakes, rapids and narrow gorges, deeper and deeper into the abyss of the north."

RIGHT: The caption for this photograph reads: "Two men standing next to 'primeval ox head' and 'mastodon tusk' in museum setting with other bones and artifacts." They were "found on Hunker Creek, 45 feet underground," according to the captions written right on the photograph. In 1897 the *New York Times* reported "rich strikes" of gold on Hunker Creek. No doubt, while digging for gold these ancient skeletal remains were unearthed.

OPPOSITE: Prospectors waiting for the wind to rise so that they can set out for the gold fields, Lake Laberge, 1897.

DANGER!
Trains and Locomotives traveling at high rate of speed pass through this Tunnel. These Trains and Locomotives have Right-of-way at all times. Entrance to this Tunnel absolutely prohibited to all, except such Employees as are employed on Tunnel. Track Repair and Maintenance work.
ALASKA JUNEAU GOLD MINING CO.

DANGER
LIVE WIRE

JUNEAU END OF TUNNEL
1242 LNP

BEFORE REACHING JUNEAU, *the Queen proceeded up the Taku Inlet that the passengers might see the fine glacier at its head, and ventured to within half a mile of the berg-discharging front, which is about three quarters of a mile wide. Bergs fell but seldom, perhaps one in half an hour. The glacier makes a rapid descent near the front. The inlet, therefore, will not be much extended beyond its present limit by the recession of the glacier. The grand rocks on either side of its channel show ice-action in telling style. The Norris Glacier, about two miles below the Taku, is a good example of a glacier in the first stage of decadence. The Taku River enters the head of the inlet a little to the east of the glaciers, coming from beyond the main coast range. All the tourists are delighted at seeing a grand glacier in the flesh. The scenery is very fine here and in the channel at Juneau. On Douglas Island there is a large mill of 240 stamps, all run by one small water-wheel, which, however, is acted on by water at enormous pressure. The forests around the mill are being rapidly nibbled away. Wind is here said to be very violent at times, blowing away people and houses and sweeping scud far up the mountain-side. Winter snow is seldom more than a foot or two deep.*

JOHN MUIR, 1916

# JUNEAU
# TREADWELL GOLD MINE

OPPOSITE, TOP: The Treadwell gold mine ran five hundred feet under the ocean on Douglas Island, near Juneau. Carpenter-turned-miner John Treadwell found a rich lode and stealthily bought up as many of the surrounding stakes as he could, expanding the mine to become the largest gold mine on earth at the time. It produced over 3 million troy ounces of gold in its forty years of operation. In 1917, the year after this picture was taken, it collapsed and filled with seawater. As it collapsed, geysers of salt water shot two hundred feet in the air out of the mine shaft. Luckily, everyone got out safely.

OPPOSITE, BOTTOM: The Alaska-Juneau gold mine was the first gold strike in Juneau, the first town established after the American purchase of Alaska. Joe Juneau was one of two miners sent out to investigate a report of gold brought in by a Tlingit chief interested in the promised reward of a hundred Hudson Bay blankets. This photograph must be later than 1914, from the date carved into the upright under the "Danger" sign.

TOP: Prospectors in Dyea, 1897. The photograph was taken by Winter & Pond. Lloyd Valentine Winter (1866–1945) and Edwin Percy Pond (1872–1943) were prominent Alaskan photographers who operated their

Juneau-based curio and photography studio for over 50 years.

ABOVE: Chilkat Indians in dancing costumes; this photograph is also by Winter & Pond. The caption reads: "Seven Chilkat Indian men and boys posed, standing, full length, in native dress."

NEITHER THE AMERICANS NOR THE RUSSIANS SAW FIT *to invite the "aboriginal element" to be present at the ceremonies. For one, I regretted the omission. How they regarded it I know not, but as the steamship John L. Stephens lay opposite the Indian portion of the town, the transit of the military could not fail to attract their notice. It is not a trait of the red man to manifest curiosity, but they were not disposed to permit the imposing ceremonies of this occasion to pass unobserved. They put off in their canoes, rounded the shipping and took a position in the harbor where they could have a distant and yet impressive view of the ceremonies. Years ago the conduct of American whalemen had made them inimical to our flag, but since the arrival of our ships-of-war in the harbor, two months ago, the four-fold price paid them by our people for venison and wild fowl had rendered them complacent. They were undetermined whether to rejoice at or regret the event. They silently watched the descending and the ascending flag, listened unmoved to the thunder of the artillery, and slowly paddled their skiffs to their own moorings.*

THE NEW YORK TIMES, DECEMBER 30, 1867

SITKA

ABOVE LEFT: Fishing boats, possibly in the port of Sitka, Alaska. Fishing was a major Alaskan industry. The large vessel on the right is the expedition ship *George W. Elder*, which carried the Edward Henry Harriman family and other members of the expedition to Alaska in 1899. The photograph was taken by Edward S. Curtis.

ABOVE RIGHT: The steamer *Topeka* at Muir Glacier in Alaska, on September 25, 1895. The passengers were promenading on shore and sitting in rowboats. This was a year before the discovery of gold triggered the great Klondike gold rush.

OPPOSITE: Tourists being photographed next to a totem pole outside of Sitka, Alaska, 1910–20.

## BIBLIOGRAPHY

### Travelers' Accounts and Literary Descriptions

Audouard, Olympe. *À travers l'Amérique, le Far West*. Paris: Imprimerie Raçon et Cie, 1869.

Crane, Stephen. *Maggie, A Girl of the Streets*. New York: Bantam Classics, 1986.

Dickens, Charles. *American Notes for General Circulation*. London: Chapman and Hall, 1863.

Dos Passos, John. *USA: The 42nd Parallel, 1919, The Big Money*. New York: Library of America, 1996.

Ferber, Edna. *Saratoga Trunk*. Garden City, NY: Doubleday Doran & Co., Inc., 1941.

Ferber, Edna. *Show Boat*. New York: Grosset & Dunlap, 1926.

Fitzgerald, F. Scott. *The Great Gatsby*. New York: Scribner Classics, 1992.

Fitzroy, Yvonne. *A Canadian Panorama*. Cookhill, Worcestershire, UK: Read Country Books, 2006.

Hesse Wartegg, Ernst von, *Nord-Amerika, seine Städte und Naturwunder, sein Land und seine Leute*, vol. 4. Leipzig: Weigel, 1880.

Hübner, Joseph Alexander. *A Ramble Round the World*, trans. Mary Elizabeth (A'Court), Lady Herbert. London: Macmillan and Co., 1874.

Hughes, Jim. *The Birth of a Century*. London and New York: Tauris Parke Books, 1994.

Huret, Jules. *En Amérique. De New York à La Nouvelle-Orléans*. Paris: Bibliothèque Charpentier, Eugène Fasquelle Éditeur, 1917.

Huret, Jules. *L'Amérique moderne*. Paris: Pierre Laffitte et Cie Éditeurs, 1911.

Huret, Jules. *En Amérique. De San Francisco au Canada*. Paris: Bibliothèque Charpentier, Eugène Fasquelle Éditeur, 1908.

Jackson, William Henry. *Time Exposure: The Autobiography of William Henry Jackson*. Albuquerque, New Mexico: University of New Mexico Press, 1986.

Johnson, Stanley, and Phyllis Shapiro. *Once Upon a Time: The Story of Boca Raton*. Florida: Arvida Corporation, 1987.

Keeler, Charles Augustus, and Louise Mapes Bunnell Keeler. *Southern California*. Los Angeles: Passenger Dept., Santa Fé Route, 1898.

King, Grace Elizabeth. *New Orleans: The Place and the People*. London: Macmillan and Co., 1896.

Kolb, Ellsworth Leonardson, and Emory Clifford Kolb. *Through the Grand Canyon from Wyoming to Mexico*. New York: Macmillan Company, 1914.

Lee, James Wideman. *The Geography of Genius*. New York: Fleming H. Revell, 1920.

Lewis, Sinclair. *Main Street*. New York: New American Library, 1989.

London, Jack. *Burning Daylight*. New York: The Macmillan Company, 1915.

Morand, Paul. *New York*, trans. Hamish Miles. New York: Book League of America/Henry Holt, 1930.

Muir, John. *Steep Trails: California, Utah, Nevada, Washington, Oregon, the Grand Cañon*, ed. William Frederic Badè. Boston: Houghton Mifflin Company, 1918.

Muir, John, and Marion Randall Parsons. *The Writings of John Muir: Travels in Alaska*, ed. William Frederic Badè. Boston: Houghton Mifflin, 1917.

Murchie, Guy. *Song of the Sky*. Cambridge, Massachusetts: Riverside Press, 1954.

Spragge, Mrs. Arthur. *From Ontario to the Pacific by C.P.R.* Toronto: C. Blackett Robinson, 1887.

Sweetser, Moses Foster. *New England: A Handbook for Travellers*, 7th ed. Boston: James R. Osgood and Co., 1881.

Verne, Jules. *The Floating City*. New York: Scribner, Armstrong, 1875.

Whitman, Walt. *Walt Whitman's Diary in Canada: With Extracts from Other of His Diaries and Literary Note-books*, ed. William Sloane Kennedy. Boston: Small, Maynard & Company, 1904.

### Histories

Cruise, David, and Alison Griffiths. *Lords of the Line, The Men Who Built the CPR*. Ontario: Penguin Books Canada Ltd, 1988.

Donzel, Catherine, and Alexis Gregory. *Grand American Hotels*. New York: Vendome Press, 1990.

Hart, E. J. *The Selling of Canada: The CPR and the Beginnings of Canadian Tourism*. Banff: Altitude Publishing Ltd, 1983.

Robinson, Bart. *Banff Springs: The Story of a Hotel*. Banff: Summerthought, 1973.

Roz, Firmin. *L'histoire du Canada, 1534–1934*. Paris: Paul Hartmann Éditeur, 1934.

Stein, Mark. *How the States Got Their Shapes*. New York: Smithsonian Books/HarperCollins, 2008.

Whyte, Jon, and Carole Harmon. *Lake Louise: A Diamond in the Wilderness*. Banff: Altitude Publishing Ltd, 1982.

### Online Reference Sources

Library and Archives Canada
www.collectionscanada.gc.ca

Library of Congress
www.loc.gov

Early Canadiana On line
www.canadiana.org

Historica—The Canadian Encyclopedia
www.thecanadianencyclopedia.com

### Guides

*Baedeker, États-Unis*. Paris: Les Guides Bleus, Hachette, 1983.

*Canada*. Paris: Guide Bleu, Hachette, 1989.

*Canada Ouest & Ontario*. Paris: Guide du Routard, Hachette, 1997–98.

*National Geographic Guide to the National Parks of the United States*, 6th ed. Washington, D.C.: National Geographic, 2009.

*National Geographic Guide to Scenic Highways and Byways*, 3rd ed. Washington, D.C.: National Geographic, 2007.

*New York: The City That Never Sleeps*. New York: Smithmark, 1994.

*San Francisco: City by the Bay*. New York: Smithmark, 1994.

### General Reference Works

*Encyclopaedia Britannica*, 13th edition.

Gunther, John. *Inside USA*, 50th anniversary edition. New York: Book-of-the-Month Club, 1997.

Krieger, Michael. *Where Rails Meet the Sea: America's Connections Between Ship and Train*. New York: MetroBooks, 1998.

Reck, Franklin M. *The Romance of American Transportation*. New York: Thomas Y. Crowell, 1938.

Henry Jacob Winser. *The Great Northwest: A Guidebook and Itinerary for the Use of Tourists and Travellers Over the Lines of the Northern Pacific Railroad, the Oregon Railway and Navigation Company and the Oregon and California Railroad . . . with Map and Many Illustrations*. New York: G. P. Putnam's Sons, 1883.

Yard, Robert Sterling. *The Book of the National Parks*. New York: Charles Scribner's Sons, 1919.

# LITERARY SOURCES

p. 25
Thomas Starr King, *The White Hills: Their Legends, Landscape, and Poetry* (1859; Boston: Estes and Lauriat, 1887), pp. 319, 325.

p. 29
Moses Foster Sweetser, *New England: A Handbook for Travellers,* 7th ed. (1873; Boston: James R. Osgood and Co., 1881), pp. 8–9.

p. 33
Franz Kafka, *Amerika,* trans. Edwin Muir (New York: New Directions, 1946), 111–12.

p. 37
Paul Morand, *New York,* trans. Hamish Miles (New York: Book League of America/Henry Holt, 1930), pp. 159–63.

p. 40
Paul Morand, *New York,* trans. Hamish Miles (New York: Book League of America/Henry Holt, 1930), pp. 46–48.

p. 42
F. Scott Fitzgerald, *The Great Gatsby* (1925; New York: Scribner Classics, 1992), 60.

p. 46
Edna Ferber, *Saratoga Trunk* (Garden City, New York: Doubleday, Doran & Company, Inc., 1941), pp. 153–54, 196–97.

p. 48
Passenger Department of the Grand Trunk Railway Company, *Pen and Sunlight Sketches of Scenery Reached by the Grand Trunk Railway* (1895).

p. 52
Mrs. Schuyler Van Rensselaer, *Niagara: A Description* (New York: Gilliss Bros., 1901), p. 1.

p. 56
Christopher Morley, *Travels in Philadelphia* (Philadelphia: David McKay Co., 1920), pp. 190–91.

p. 60
Herbert Russell, *The New York Times,* 8 June 1947.

p. 65
Joseph Alexander Hübner, *A Ramble Round the World,* trans. Mary Elizabeth (A'Court), Lady Herbert (1871; London: Macmillan and Co., 1874), pp. 32–33.

p. 70
James Wideman Lee, *The Geography of Genius* (New York: Fleming H. Revell, 1920), pp. 233–34.

p. 74
Julia Collier Harris, *The Life and Letters of Joel Chandler Harris* (Boston: Houghton Mifflin Company, 1918), pp. 255–56.

p. 79
Morrie Riskind, from the screenplay of *The Cocoanuts* (Paramount Pictures, 1929; adapted from George S. Kaufman's script for the Broadway play of the same name, 1925).

p. 83
Stanley Johnson and Phyllis Shapiro, *Once Upon a Time: The Story of Boca Raton* (Florida: Arvida Corporation, 1987), pp. 9–10.

p. 90
François-René Chateaubriand, *Travels in America,* trans. Richard Switzer (1791; Lexington, Kentucky: University of Kentucky Press, 1969), pages 13–14.

p. 92
Joseph Alexander Hübner, *A Ramble Round the World,* trans. Mary Elizabeth (A'Court), Lady Herbert (1871; London: Macmillan and Co., 1874), pp. 49–50, 55.

p. 97
James Fenimore Cooper, *The Oak-Openings: or, The Bee-Hunter* (New York: D. Appleton & Company, 1881), pp. 491–92.

p. 100
Jim Harrison, *True North: A Novel* (New York: Grove Press, 2004), p. 20.

p. 105
Joseph Alexander Hübner, *A Ramble Round the World,* trans. Mary Elizabeth (A'Court), Lady Herbert (1871; London: Macmillan and Co., 1874), pp. 68–69.

p. 108
Charles Dickens, *American Notes for General Circulation* (London: Chapman and Hall, 1863), p. 112.

p. 112
Kate Chopin, *At Fault* (1890; Knoxville, Tennessee: University of Tennessee Press, 2001), pp. 40–41.

p. 116
Edward King, "The Great South: Among the Mountains of Western North Carolina," in *Scribners Monthly,* vol. 7, no. 5, March 1874, pp. 514, 522.

p. 118
*United States Supreme Court Reports* (Rochester, New York: The Lawyers' Co-Operative Publishing Company, 1901), p. 691.

p. 122
Margaret Mitchell, *Gone with the Wind* (New York: Macmillan Company, 1938), pp. 849–50.

p. 127
Grace Elizabeth King, *New Orleans: The Place and the People* (London: Macmillan and Co., 1896), pp. 340–41.

p. 131
Laura F. Hinsdale, "Celebrated Men of the Day. II. Charles Gayarré, the Southern Historian," *Belford's Monthly,* 1890, p. 882.

p. 139
F. Scott Fitzgerald, *The Great Gatsby* (1925; New York: Scribner Classics, 1992), pp. 150–51.

p. 140
Sinclair Lewis, *Main Street* (1920; New York: New American Library, 1989), pp. 18, 21–22.

p. 145
Theodore Roosevelt, *Hunting Trips of a Ranchman: Sketches of Sport on the Northern Cattle Plains* (New York: G. P. Putnam's Sons, 1886), pp. 175–76.

p. 146
William Frederick Cody, *An Autobiography of Buffalo Bill* (New York: Cosmopolitan Book Corporation, 1920), pp. 277–78.

p. 150
William Henry Jackson, *Time Exposure: The Autobiography of William Henry Jackson* (1940; Albuquerque, New Mexico: University of New Mexico Press, 1986), pp. 197–98.

p. 155
George Bird Grinnell, "The Crown of the Continent," in *The Century Illustrated Monthly Magazine,* vol. 62, 1901, p. 660.

p. 158
Francis Potter Daniels, *The Flora of Boulder, Colorado, and Vicinity,* (Columbia, Missouri: The University of Missouri, 1911), pp. 1–7.

p. 162
Olympe Audouard, *À travers l'Amérique, le Far West* (Paris: Imprimerie Simon Raçon et Cie., 1869), pp. 105–6.

p. 166
William Henry Jackson *Time Exposure: The Autobiography of William Henry Jackson* (1940; Albuquerque, New Mexico: University of New Mexico Press, 1986), p. 216.

p. 168
David Sievert Lavender, *One Man's West* (1943; Lincoln, Nebraska: University of Nebraska Press, 1977), pp. 3–4.

p. 172
Willa Cather, *Death Comes for the Archbishop* (1927; Lincoln, Nebraska: University of Nebraska Press, 1999), pp. 282–83.

p. 176
*The New York Times,* 22 December 1890.

p. 179
Percival Lowell, *Mars as the Abode of Life,* (New York: Macmillan Company, 1908), p. 125.

p. 183
Ellsworth Leonardson Kolb and Emory Clifford Kolb, *Through the Grand Canyon from Wyoming to Mexico* (New York: Macmillan Company, 1914), p. 205.

p. 186
Robert Sterling Yard, *The Book of the National Parks* (New York: Charles Scribner's Sons, 1919), p. 357.

p. 188
John Muir *Steep Trails: California, Utah, Nevada, Washington, Oregon, the Grand Cañon,* ed. William Frederic Badè (1877; Boston: Houghton Mifflin Company, 1918), p. 107.

p. 192
Anne O'Hare McCormick, *The New York Times,* 1 November 1931.

p. 196
Jack Kerouac, *On the Road* (1957; New York: Penguin Classics, 2003), p. 60.

p. 204
Annette Fitch-Brewer, *The Story of a Mother-Love* (Akron, Ohio: New Werner Company, 1913), pp. 166–68.

p. 206
John Muir *Steep Trails: California, Utah, Nevada, Washington, Oregon, the Grand Cañon,* ed. William Frederic Badè (1889; Boston: Houghton Mifflin Company, 1918), p. 261.

p. 208
Henry Jacob Winser, *The Great Northwest: A Guidebook and Itinerary for the Use of Tourists and Travellers Over the Lines of the Northern Pacific Railroad, the Oregon Railway and Navigation Company and the Oregon and California Railroad . . . with Map and Many Illustrations* (New York: G. P. Putnam's Sons, 1883), pp. 242–43.

p. 213
Franklin D. Roosevelt, "Address at Timberline Lodge," speech delivered on 29 September 1937, in *The Works of Franklin D. Roosevelt;* reprinted in *The Public Papers and Addresses of Franklin D. Roosevelt,* 1937 volume (New York: Macmillan Company, 1941), p. 392.

p. 214
Miriam McGuire, "Taking a Timber Claim," *The Overland Monthly,* vol. 66, no. 1, 1915, p. 155.

p. 217
Frona Eunice Wait, *The Kingship of Mt. Lassen: At Present the Only Active Volcano on the Mainland of the United States, in the Past California's Greatest Benefactor* (San Francisco: Nemo Publishing Co., 1922), p. 32.

p. 220
Joseph Alexander Hübner, *A Ramble Round the World,* trans. Mary Elizabeth (A'Court), Lady Herbert (1871; London: Macmillan and Co., 1874), p. 163.

p. 223
Galen Clark, *Indians of the Yosemite Valley and Vicinity: Their History, Customs and Traditions* (Yosemite Valley, California: G. Clark, 1904), pp. 101–2.

p. 228
Laura Ingalls Wilder, *West from Home: Letters of Laura Ingalls Wilder to Almanzo Wilder, San Francisco, 1915*, ed. Roger Lea MacBride (New York: Harper & Row, 1974), p. 44.

p. 230
Joseph Alexander Hübner, *A Ramble Round the World*, trans. Mary Elizabeth (A'Court), Lady Herbert (1871; London: Macmillan and Co., 1874), p. 154.

p. 235
Walter Hines Page and Arthur Wilson Page, *The World's Work: A History of Our Time* (New York: Doubleday, Doran and Co., Inc., 1902), p. 2,426.

p. 239
John Muir, *Steep Trails: California, Utah, Nevada, Washington, Oregon, the Grand Cañon*, ed. William Frederic Badè (1877; Boston: Houghton Mifflin Company, 1918), p. 136.

p. 242
Charles Augustus Keeler and Louise Mapes Bunnell Keeler, *Southern California* (Los Angeles: Passenger Dept., Santa Fé Route, 1898), pp. 53–59.

p. 246
*The New York Times*, 29 August 1911.

p. 251
Charles Augustus Keeler and Louise Mapes Bunnell Keeler, *Southern California* (Los Angeles: Passenger Dept., Santa Fé Route, 1898), p. 63.

p. 254
Charles Augustus Keeler and Louise Mapes Bunnell Keeler, *Southern California* (Los Angeles: Passenger Dept., Santa Fé Route, 1898), pp. 97–99.

p. 262
Walt Whitman, *Walt Whitman's Diary in Canada: With Extracts from Other of His Diaries and Literary Note-books*, ed. William Sloane Kennedy (Boston: Small, Maynard & Company, 1904), p. 27.

p. 266
George Johnson, *Canada, Its History, Productions and Natural Resources: The Universal and International Exhibition, Liége, 1905*, ed. Sydney Arthur Fisher (Ottawa: Department of Agriculture of Canada, 1905), p. 93.

p. 270
Walt Whitman, *Walt Whitman's Diary in Canada: With Extracts from Other of His Diaries and Literary Note-books*, ed. William Sloane Kennedy (Boston: Small, Maynard & Company, 1904), pp. 28–34.

p. 273
Yvonne Fitzroy, *A Canadian Panorama* (1929; Cookhill, Worcestershire, UK: Read Country Books, 2006), pp. 92–93.

p. 274
Yvonne Fitzroy, *A Canadian Panorama* (1929; Cookhill, Worcestershire, UK: Read Country Books, 2006), pp. 96–97.

p. 279
James Lumsden, *Through Canada in Harvest Time: A Study of Life and Labour in the Golden West* (London: T. F. Unwin, 1903), pp. 78–79.

p. 283
Gertrude E. Benham, "The Ascent of Mt. Assiniboine," in *Canadian Alpine Journal* (Winnipeg, Manitoba: Alpine Club of Canada, 1907), pp. 93–94.

p. 286
John Wilton Cuninghame Haldane, *3800 Miles Across Canada* (London: Simpkin, Marshall, Hamilton, Kent & Co., 1908), pp. 186–87.

p. 291
Yvonne Fitzroy, *A Canadian Panorama* (1929; Cookhill, Worcestershire, UK: Read Country Books, 2006), pp. 161–62.

p. 294
Mrs. Arthur Spragge, *From Ontario to the Pacific by the C.P.R.* (Toronto: C. B. Robinson, 1887), pp. 62–63.

p. 297
Roselle Theodore Cross, *My Mountains* (Boston: The Stratford Co., 1921), pp. 148–50.

p. 299
Mrs. Arthur Spragge, *From Ontario to the Pacific by the C.P.R.* (Toronto: C. B. Robinson, 1887), p. 169.

p. 303
Arthur Granville Bradley, *Canada in the Twentieth Century* (London: A. Constable, 1905), pp. 279–80.

p. 307
John Charles Van Dyke, *The Mountain: Renewed Studies in Impressions and Appearances* (New York: Charles Scribner's Sons, 1916), pp. 152–53.

Page 308
Jack London, *Burning Daylight* (New York: The Macmillan Company, 1915), pages 51–52.

Page 311
John Muir and Marion Randall Parsons, *The Writings of John Muir: Travels in Alaska*, ed. William Frederic Badè (Boston: Houghton Mifflin, 1917), pp. 334–35.

Page 312
Correspondent of the *Boston Journal*, Sitka, District of Alaska, 30 December 1867, in the *New York Times*.

## PHOTOGRAPHIC CREDITS

The documents and photographs reproduced in this volume are part of the Marc Walter collection, with the exception of those listed below, with their sources.

Anil Sharma: pp. 192 (bottom), 248–49; © Blog da Rua Nove: p. 11 (top); Collection Cailly: pp. 137 (bottom), 186 (right); Catherine Donzel: pp. 262, 288–89; Frashers Fotos Collection: pp. 244–45; David Rumsey Collection: pp. 12–13; Matthew R. Isenburg Collection: p. 168 (bottom); Corbis: pp. 226–27 (Morton Beebe), 278 (Christopher Morris); Courtesy of Christopher Cardozo: pp. 256–57; San Francisco Maritime National Historical Park: pp. 198–99, 224–25, 232–33, 240–41, 252–53; Marc Walter (photographs): pp. 30, 31, 205; Photoglob AG, Zurich: pp. 6, 15 (2nd from the top), 16 (center), 24 (bottom), 48 (top left and right), 49, 56 (left), 60 (top), 68–69, 84–85, 87 (center), 104, 126 (top and bottom right), 127, 128–29, 135 (bottom), 150 (top), 151, 179, 202 (top), 235 (bottom), 242 (top left), 254 (bottom), 295, 296 (top), 297; Library of Congress, Prints and Photographs Division, Washington, D.C.: pp. 1, 4, 5, 7 (right), 8–9, 10, 11 (bottom right), 12 (bottom), 14, 15 (top, center, and 2nd from bottom), 17, 21 (bottom), 22 (top 3 images), 23 (top), 29 (top right), 32 (top left and right), 36, 40, 41, 42 (right), 43 (top), 46, 48 (bottom), 52 (left), 62–63, 64 (bottom), 71 (bottom), 74 (bottom), 76–77, 78, 87 (2nd from the top), 88–89, 97 (left), 98–99, 101 (bottom), 102–3, 108 (right), 110 (bottom left), 112, 114–15, 116, 117 (top), 118–19 (top), 120–21, 126 (bottom left), 135 (top 2 images), 136, 137 (top 4 images), 138, 139 (right), 140 (top left and bottom), 142–43, 145, 146 (bottom), 152–53, 154, 154–55 (top), 158, 159 (bottom left), 169, 170, 171, 172 (bottom), 173, 174–75, 178, 182, 183 (bottom), 186 (left), 194–95, 196–97, 201 (bottom), 203 (center), 204, 206, 207, 208 (bottom), 208–9 (top), 214–15, 216, 217, 220 (right and bottom), 223 (top), 228 (bottom left and right), 236–37, 238 (left), 246 (top), 250–51 (top), 260, 264–65, 270 (left), 304–5, 306–7, 308–9, 310–11, 312–13.

## ACKNOWLEDGMENTS

Antony Shugaar wishes to dedicate this book to the three people in his life without whom he could not have written this book or any other: Arlie, Gerda, and Lisa. He would also like to thank Marc Walter, Catherine Donzel, and Sabine Arqué.

The creation of this book was made possible through the assistance and generosity of a great many people, especially Christopher Cardozo, Henry Golas, and David Rumsey.

In particular, Catherine Donzel would like to thank her friend Patrick Lévy.

Sabine Arqué would like to express her appreciation to Dominique Bourgois, Olivier Colette, Boris Danzer-Kantof, Philippe Rollet, Florence Cailly, Émilie Boismoreau, and Anna Lébédeff.

Last of all, Éditions du Chêne would like to thank Mark Magowan for his support and his generous assistance.

First published in the United States of America in 2009 by
The Vendome Press
1334 York Avenue
New York, NY 10021
www.vendomepress.com

Originally published in 2008 by Éditions du Chêne as *Voyages en Amérique du Nord* under the direction of Marc Walter
Authors: Catherine Donzel and Antony Shugaar

Copyright © 2008 Éditions du Chêne – Hachette Livre
This edition copyright © 2009 The Vendome Press

ISBN 978-0-86565-259-0

Concept and art direction: Marc Walter / Chine
Additional editing and picture research: Sabine Arqué / Florence Cailly / Chine
Mapmaker: Caroline Seigle
Photogravure: PPS

Editor, English-language edition: Jacqueline Decter
Type designer, English-language edition: Patricia Fabricant

Library of Congress Cataloging-in-Publication Data

Shugaar, Antony.
  Coast to coast : vintage travel in North America / by Antony Shugaar, Marc
Walter, Catherine Donzel.
    p. cm.
  ISBN 978-0-86565-259-0
  1. Travel—United States—History. 2. Transportation—United States—History. 3. United States—Description and travel.  I. Walter, Marc. II. Donzel, Catherine. III. Title.

  HE203.S54 2009
  306.4'819097309041—dc22

                                        2009013318

Printed in Malaysia
First printing

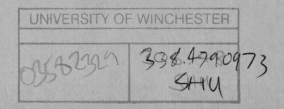